Development of Federal Legislation for Vocational Education

The Authors: *Upper Left*, Layton S. Hawkins; *Right*, Charles A. Prosser;
Lower Left, John C. Wright

Development of Federal Legislation for Vocational Education

Compiled by

J. Chester Swanson
Professor of Education
University of California

Compiled from DEVELOPMENT OF VO-
CATIONAL EDUCATION by Hawkins,
Prosser and Wright. With additional material covering legislation from 1947 to
the present in Chapters IX and X by the
compiler.

AMERICAN TECHNICAL SOCIETY
CHICAGO, ILLINOIS 60637

PREFACE

The story of the early development of federal legislation for vocational education in the public schools of the United States revolves around a relatively few educators and legislators who worked for many years to create a workable program and to obtain its acceptance. Layton S. Hawkins, Charles A. Prosser and John C. Wright were among the most influential persons in the development and the early administration of vocational education. We are thus dealing with source material when we read the story of vocational education legislation and its administration as described by these authors in their book, *Development of Vocational Education,* written in 1951.

This publication is a compilation from several chapters of the text by Hawkins, Prosser and Wright with material added to bring the story of federal legislation up to the present. A compilation was first written in 1961 for the Panel of Consultants on Vocational Education to be used by that committee for its deliberations concerning recommendations for additional federal legislation. The material was made available for the general public by the publisher. This is a further revision carrying the story of federal legislation through the 89th Congress, First Session—December, 1965.

It is, of course, very difficult to select 93 pages from a book of 656 pages and not violate some of the elements of good composition—e.g., emphasis, coherence and unity. As these violations occur they should be credited to the compiler and not the original authors.

The period of active service of the authors of the original text has ended. Their achievements are well known and continue to be an inspiration to those who were privileged to know them. If this publication makes it possible to improve the effectiveness of vocational education, it will serve the objectives the authors had in mind when they wrote their original volume.

The compiler is indebted to Walter Arnold, Assistant Commissioner, United States Office of Education and his staff of the Division of Vocational and Technical Education for assistance and research.

J. CHESTER SWANSON,
Professor of Education,
University of California, Berkeley

CONTENTS

CHAPTER I

Historic Background of Vocational Education

VOCATIONAL EDUCATION AND A CHANGING CIVILIZATION

Vocational education made very early beginnings among the races of mankind. In all man's effort to conquer his physical environment—the dangers and rigors of the external world—manual skill and knowledge pertinent to specific tasks have in one way or another been transmitted from man to man and from generation to generation.

Each time a new discovery increased by the smallest amount the store of knowledge held by man, it became necessary to disseminate that knowledge and put it to use. This was done by developing skills among recruits to the arts.

In a primitive and static society there was no wealth of usable knowledge upon which to draw when man pondered better ways of doing things and means of easing burdens. Discoveries were rare and invention so slow that man could only inch his way toward a better and safer existence. But even in this groping "progress," the usual or customary occupations and work processes had somehow to be taught succeeding generations. Most of the skill and knowledge handed down from one generation to the next had been traditional among the races for centuries.[1]

Vocational Education and the Social Recruit. It is probable that all the phenomena of vocational training existing in modern society have their roots in the past. In one sense, at least, we are not dealing with a new thing, but with extensions and developments of a system of training long in use.

Youth, in all ages, has been looked upon as an invaluable asset to the social unit, whether that unit comprised the family or the state. This idea stems from the concern of man for his security. Undoubtedly the first objective of vocational training was to develop skill in using weapons. With weapons man obtained food for himself and his family; with weapons he confronted his enemies. Group

[1] Prosser and Allen, *Vocational Education in a Democracy* (New York: Appleton-Century, 1925); rev. ed. (Chicago: American Technical Society, 1949).

1

safety being vital, this kind of training was possibly the first to take conscious and organized form. Moreover, training in the use of weapons is probably one of the oldest activities of the teaching profession.

Next in importance from the standpoints of social survival and progress was the gaining of an appreciation of youth as a resource of the future—a labor asset; hence recognition of the need to give what may rightly be called vocational education to social recruits. Education of this kind appears early in human history.

Vocational Education in the Family. Vocational training in its early aspects seems to have adopted one or the other of two procedures, the training of youth being accomplished either as a natural outcome of family living or by studious observance of the art and practices of adult members of the social group. By the latter procedure youth learned through imitation. On the whole, the training a youth received in "productive" tasks—such as tilling the soil and caring for domestic animals—was secured from the male members of the family. For skill in the use of weapons, the youth coming into manhood had the benefit of instruction from huntsmen and warriors, the valiant members of the tribe performing this duty in the way of custom.

In the primitive stage of human endeavor there was little ease, but only unremitting hard work, and most tasks were "work tasks." Then, as always, certain members of the group evinced singular ability in the performance of this or that task. Occasionally, whether by diligence or happenstance, someone would discover a new and more efficient way of doing a certain thing, or perhaps make a startling discovery. In either case, it was the custom to assign young members of the group to those skilled in the arts practiced by the elders—hunting, fishing, and fighting, or the practices employed in yielding products from the soil—that these recruits to all the skills upon which man based his security might themselves acquire skill. This education of youth in earliest times and among all peoples formed the basis of the "helper" system of modern employment.

Present Stage of Development. We still have, and probably always will have, in modern society all the forms of vocational education above described. Farm boys still learn farming from their fathers. At the same time, agricultural schools and colleges are making great strides in the systematic teaching of agriculture to growing numbers. Girls still learn the duties of housekeeping from their mothers, nevertheless organized instruction in home economics has become an increasingly important part of curricula in schools throughout the land.

Even today, countless workers in widely diversified fields learn their jobs by pickup methods, in which observation, imitation, and individual initiative constitute the sole means of training. However, increasing opportunities to secure organized training are being offered by employers, by schools, by skilled craftsmen, and by all agencies concerned with industrial improvement.

The generally accepted principle that only a person who is himself competent in a craft can give effective vocational instruction in that craft asserts the value of the specialist in transmitting skill and knowledge. Every discovery of the world of science and every invention finds its use through instruction given to others by its discoverer. Only in this way does any discovery add to the sum of human knowledge and achievement.

As civilization has developed, the tendency has been to increase the educational area covered by conscious and more or less organized instruction to the furthest possible extent. This has long been the case in academic education, and it is likewise the case in vocational education. In general the whole problem of education—in civilized society as compared with the static society of primitive peoples—is one involving factors of individual initiative and ingenuity; unconscious absorption and imitation; conscious imitation in the home; unorganized training in the home; organized training in the home; division between home and occupation; conscious and organized training through apprenticeship; pickup learning of specialized tasks; and organized training through such devices as apprenticeship, the foreman instructor, and the public and private vocational school.

Modern Conditions and Vocational Training. The tremendous expansion of production caused by the substitution of the power-driven machine for the old handcrafts, and the resulting keener competition of modern business, require more rapid and more effective training of larger numbers of people. In the face of this demand the ineffectiveness and inadequacy of the pickup method of training new workers have gradually become apparent.

The contributions of science and invention have not only made this tremendous production possible but have called increasingly for systematic training of technicians and leaders. The progress of science and invention has resulted in an increased demand for the technician and inventor and, at the same time, has created great numbers of new jobs and profoundly modified the processes of many old jobs.

On the whole, the content of an industrial occupation easiest to secure by pickup and practice is manipulative skill. However, the demand for manipulative skill *only* has shifted to a demand for technical knowledge as well (the *why* of the *how*), and the ability to apply that knowledge intelligently. As this shift has occurred, it has become necessary to equip the learner with understanding and resourcefulness through some form of organized training. The realization of this has led to a renewed interest in vocational education to make it more systematic and therefore more efficient.

This increased interest has shown itself not only through establishing vocational schools under public control, but even to a more pronounced degree through such private endeavors as the revival of apprenticeship; the attempt to restore the foreman to his ancient place as instructor of his men; and the establishment of correspondence, privately endowed, and corporation schools.

A Social Efficiency Device. Social wealth furnishes the opportunity for society to maintain stability and progress. The greater the degree to which social wealth can be produced efficiently, the greater the potential resources with which to achieve our aims as a nation.

On the whole, organized vocational education is an efficiency device. It undertakes to do nothing that has not been done before. It merely strives to discharge the function more efficiently. It can, therefore, be regarded as one of the agencies whereby the state can more efficiently secure social wealth. The trend toward more systematic training is nothing more than the crude realization that this belief is true. It follows, therefore, that in proportion as we are able to substitute organized vocational education for unorganized vocational education will social progress be furthered, will greater social wealth be produced at less cost, and will society be better equipped to carry on its struggle against destructive forces in nature, and to realize its hopes and aims.

This history tells the story of the long struggle to develop through science, discovery, and invention a dynamic, instead of a static, civilization, and to develop, also, a dynamic system of free public vocational education to support and promote that civilization.

CHAPTER II

Economic Theory of Vocational Education

Education, not force, must be relied upon to secure stability and progress in a democracy. In the preceding chapter it was pointed out that stability and progress depend upon the production of wealth through the conservation of natural and human resources. All education contributes to this conservation. Education must be adapted to a wide diversity of human needs and human problems. However, it must take many forms, each contributing in a special way to the general objective. We must consider vocational education as a special form of education in its relation to the development of the material and human assets of a people. Therefore we must consider it in its relation to the well-being of a democracy.[1]

Vocational Education and the Democratic Process. There are two ways in which vocational education functions in any forward-looking program of a democracy. First, it conserves natural resources. Second, it conserves human resources. It conserves material resources by promoting, disseminating, and transmitting skill, knowledge, and the results of invention, and by conserving human effort. It conserves human resources, not only by conserving human effort, but by promoting morale and intelligence. This chapter deals with the relation of training to the conservation of both material and human resources.

The Self-Contained Country. Wealth is created by making the most of natural resources whether these be native to a country or imported. A country having no means of importing natural resources, or no need to import them, might be called "self-contained."

In such a country the total wealth produced would depend upon the value of the products created from natural resources, in terms of consumer demand. The value of such products depends upon the amount of skill applied in turning them out. It also depends upon

---

[1] The material composing this chapter has been freely adapted from Prosser and Allen, *Vocational Education in a Democracy* (New York: The Century Co., 1925). Rev. ed. by Prosser and Quigley (Chicago: The American Technical Society, 1949).

the efficiency of the operations and processes by which production is accomplished.

In a self-contained country natural resources would be fixed. The amount of skill and technical knowledge used in creating products would be limited only by the possibilities of human invention and the extent to which skill could be developed and utilized. We can set no bounds upon the possibilities of invention, nor upon the discoveries of science. We can set no bounds upon the applications of technical knowledge, nor upon the limits of human skill. A self-contained country would gain in wealth in proportion as these factors were developed and applied.

No Country Self-Contained. In reality, however, no country is self-contained. The development of cheap methods of transportation has made it possible for any region to draw upon the natural resources of any other region. England could not exist today if it did not draw upon the natural resources of other countries. Its textile industries have assumed huge proportions in a land unable to raise a single pound of cotton or silk. This need to draw upon the resources of others is even more true of our own New England states.

The fact that any state or any nation is in competition with countries more favored in possession of this or that natural resource than itself, makes necessary the development of higher skills and greater technical knowledge to offset the advantage held by countries more favorably endowed. This fact was one of the important points considered by the Douglas Commission on Industrial Education for the state of Massachusetts. The commission's report was the chief instrument in securing a strong vocational program for that state.

Discovery and Invention Fundamental. If the wealth of any country depends upon what it is able to do with native or imported raw material, and if progress and stability depend upon the extent to which wealth is produced, then any country is vitally concerned with the means by which skill is developed, technical knowledge obtained and applied, and science and invention promoted.

The basis on which the character of skill is determined and technical knowledge secured is the development of science and invention. In this respect a democracy has a decided advantage over countries having a form of government tending to be repressive. Democracy offers the freedom of initiative that spurs the effort of scientists and inventors.

Developing Machines and Processes. Society is not only interested in the promotion of scientific discovery and invention as a means of producing wealth from natural resources. It is also interested in the efficiency with which these resources are converted into marketable products. The struggle to achieve maximum utilization of natural resources—a struggle which never ceases—passes through three stages. A discovery is made in the field of science. A new machine or mechanical appliance is invented. The problem then becomes one of working out processes and of developing the machine so that it will produce with the highest efficiency and with a minimum expenditure of time, energy, and money. During this second stage, as the machine is improved or the process involved is more fully worked out, there is need for development of the skill required to operate the machine or control the process.

In this stage there is required, from those who have full knowledge of the process and the machine, an accurate estimate of the technical knowledge required for control of the process or for operation of the machine. This knowledge constitutes the *content* of the particular production job.

Continuous Development Necessary to Progress. If we stop with the discovery itself or with the invention, either it suffers neglect or we fall far short of securing from it all the benefit to be had. If we fail to determine the kind and degree of skill needed to operate a new machine or carry on a new process as each is developed, we fail to get the greatest good from the product of our creative skill. If we fail at all stages in the development of a machine or a process to determine the nature of the knowledge required for successful operation and control of that machine or that process, then we fail to realize the ultimate in benefits to be derived.

Progressive Development. It was a fundamental discovery of the physicist Faraday that a wire cutting through lines of magnetic force induces within itself an electric current. During a period of nearly a hundred years this basic discovery, through a series of inventions, developed into the electric generator. Ever since one of the first electric generators was installed to increase electric power in a lighthouse on the English Channel, it has been required that operators of the machine possess the skill and understanding of the technical knowledge related to the tasks they perform.

Improvements have changed the construction and design of the dynamo. The kind of skill required to operate the machine also has changed. The technical knowledge which the operator needs has changed correspondingly. The development of the practical application of the Faraday discovery resulted in a continual training process whereby the necessary skill and the functioning technical knowledge made the device a serviceable machine.

The same might be said of the many mechanical devices, operating procedures, and chemical processes. All of them originated in the discovery of a simple physical or chemical phenomenon. All of them, through a long period of development, arrived at their present stage of efficiency through a process of evolution.

Adaptation of the Worker to Changing Demands. The necessity for rapid adaptation of the worker to the job, and for continuous readaptation as new machines and high-production methods are introduced, finds the pickup method, even for the unskilled, woefully inadequate to the situation. Large-scale production makes the efficiency of the worker a matter of far greater concern today than in the past. It is increasingly necessary that the old "breaking in" process of training workers be supplanted by well-organized and more systematic ways of conferring both knowledge and skill. What has been said in this regard applies especially to industrial activities. The notion that better methods of imparting knowledge and skill are less essential in agriculture, in commercial pursuits, and in activities of the home is false.

Unfortunately, the substitution of systematic for makeshift vocational training procedures is evidenced almost exclusively by the universities and engineering schools. Without intending in any way to discount the accomplishments of training below college grade for industry, agriculture, commerce, and the home, it must be admitted that the showing here is far less impressive than in the field of professional education.

In fairness it should be said that in the professional field the pickup method of training has been practically abolished. For the great mass of workers it continues in force. This difference cannot be accounted for altogether by the fact that in such professions as law and medicine and teaching legal standards have been set up which individuals are compelled to meet in order to be admitted to practice. Rather, the difference is due chiefly to the fact that the professions have traditionally been held to be dignified and important enough to merit every assistance. On the other hand, productive work, whether in agriculture or industry, has been held in lower esteem. Until recent years, those engaged in it received a more meager share of encouragement and help than was their due.

Licensing Promotes Organized Training. It is significant that in many places in this country license requirements have been established for plumbers, electricians, and steam engineers. The licensing of plumbers came about through the realization that men engaged in this field were sanitary agents whose work affects public health. The licensing of electricians came about because of the awareness of dangers to life and property of "handyman" installations of wiring and electrical devices. The same is true of work in the field of steam engineering.

The setting up of license restrictions was followed by programs of organized training planned to fit the job applicant effectively. In a reasonable length of time programs were set up to meet requirements of the state examining board, and therefore of the job. Certification of tradesmen, however, was established not for the purpose of promoting the trades or to control the training of workers, but solely as a measure in the public interest.

The old apprenticeship plan was well suited to the conditions of a simple society in which knowledge and skill were handed down from one generation to another. It failed to meet the conditions of modern society. The problem became one of disseminating as widely and as rapidly as possible the knowledge and skill that keep step with discovery and invention.

The constantly growing body of information and the resulting shift in tools and techniques taking place in industry, create a very great demand for trained workers in widely diversified fields. Means of rapid communication make it possible to spread needed knowledge effectively. It requires organized vocational education to insure that assistance shall be given in a systematic way whenever and wherever it is needed.

A scientist established absolute proof that black rust which had proved a prolific source of loss in wheat-growing regions was due to the presence of the Barberry bush, which was the source of contamination. In the fourteenth century, it would have taken a full hundred years for this information to have spread over Europe. How different it is in our time! Within twenty-four hours after proof of the source of the blight was established, the fact was known to leaders in agriculture in every state in the Union. By virtue of the speed with which this information went out to growers and others vitally interested, it took only a few months to institute measures that would combat the evil successfully. Failure to give rapid transmission to such information would have meant a large loss of potential wealth, with accompanying economic distress.

Rank and File Stewardship. So far the discussion has been directed to the problem of mass education. It has been directed to the training of the ordinary worker in the shop, in the office, on the farm, and in the home. But all that has been said applies with equal and sometimes even greater force as we go up the scale to the jobs of leadership in economic activities of every kind.

We have not thought of the engineering or the agricultural college as a vocational school. We have not realized the extent to which leadership in production is represented by men who have come up through the ranks from journeymanship to positions of responsibility. These men were without engineering education and without organized occupational training. They gained by intelligence and earnest application a mastery of the processes of control operating within their special occupational spheres. They gained, as well, the ability to organize and direct.

The "training" these men obtained was meager, unscientific, and wasteful of time and effort, but they worked to the top nevertheless. In their ranks may be found most of our great captains of industry as well as executives, superintendents, and department heads.

We have provided well in this country for the engineering technician. But we have neglected the training needs of most of the present and prospective technicians of industry. Probably no other country in the world has recognized the economic and social value of this group so clearly as has Germany. Germany has promoted its highest development by providing schools such as the *Mittel Teknikal Shule* (Middle Technical School).

As systematic vocational education is developed in this country through a wide variety of day, part-time, and evening classes for apprentices and journeymen, so will the industrial leaders of America (most of whom will continue to come from the ranks) be wisely selected and well equipped to meet the growing demands and responsibilities of their callings. Nothing else will so promote economic efficiency in America.

When the American technical high school, common to our larger cities, finds its best field of usefulness, it will not be as a preparatory school for the engineering college. That is a service which the university does not regard as necessary, since college entrance requirements stand in support of the regular high school. The technical high school will serve as a finishing school preparing young men and women for careers leading to positions of authority on the directive side of industry.

Opening the Way for the Inventor. No other country in the entire world has been so prolific in discovering and inventing ways to increase production and reduce costs as the United States. Applied to our rich natural resources, these discoveries and inventions will continue to be the chief factor in the creation of our social wealth, with its attendant opportunities for social progress. In his economic and social value, Thomas A. Edison was worth more than thousands of ordinary citizens because his inventions and discoveries created a better way of life for all mankind. Perhaps more than any other group we need to conserve the discovering scientist and the functioning inventor.

In any examination of the records of the Patent Office, and in current information, it is seen that most of the successful inventors are not technicians, but mechanics. Some inventions have been the result of accident and guesswork. The greatest number, however, are the result of earnest study and patient experiment. Usually, the inventor has brought to his task a native intelligence and a trained resourcefulness.

The inventor is also a man who has gained skill by practical experience and understanding of mechanical processes commonly employed. However, he lacks, at the beginning of the task undertaken, the special skills and the special technical knowledge necessary to solution of his difficulties. As a result he muddles his way through by a process of trial and error. He acquires through his mistakes a grasp of the technical principles and mechanical laws applicable to his problem. He may need the information of others before the device upon which he bends his efforts can be made to work successfully. Generally, all of these conditions enter the situation.

The Social Waste of Haphazard Invention. This haphazard method of learning to invent is socially wasteful even in the case of the inventor who is finally successful. He often spends years in misdirected and futile effort before he makes one contribution. If he had been properly equipped with the functioning facts bearing on his problem, the periods of blundering experimentation would have been greatly curtailed. The time saved could have been applied to the production of other inventions or to the discovery of other practical processes.

On the other hand, files of the Patent Office are cluttered with thousands of ingenious devices that, though conceived by great inventive ability, are of no value to the world. Either they will not work successfully under commercial conditions, or some vital principle affecting function was not recognized. Perhaps the device served small demand or none at all. Had the creators of these devices been aware of the principles involved, they might have been spared long hours of vain endeavor and the disheartenment of profitless labors.

The records of the Patent Office, however, do not tell of the thousands of would-be inventors who attempt to burst upon the world with new devices, but have wasted their efforts because of ignorance of physical facts and principles unalterably involved. Knowledge of these matters would have prevented earnest and keenly able individuals from working to no purpose in defiance of fixed principles of the physical world.

Records furnish no information about still other able persons whose ideas never take shape in any workable device or process. They became disheartened because they lacked technical knowledge or because inadequate skill and the lack of opportunity to acquire these assets kept them from success.

Vocational Education and Invention. If it were possible to establish successful schools for the training of inventors at public expense, the enterprise would probably be the wisest social investment that could be made, regardless of cost. There is no such thing as direct training for the "occupation" of inventing—none that the authors are aware of, at least. Like poets, inventors are born, and not made. They possess certain native aptitudes that create successfully in proportion to the experience of resourceful thinking in respect to devices and processes. So this aptitude has been equipped in some way with the thinking stuff—the experiences, the skill, and the pertinent information which are needed to solve problems.

As organized vocational education comes to take the place of the old pickup method of the past, this thinking stuff will be so diffused that every person having inventive abilities will have the opportunity to get the help he now so badly needs. This will be sure to result in uncovering and selecting, stimulating and equipping better invention. It will lead to the creation of better devices and processes for the conservation of human effort in the production of social wealth.

Organized Invention. The recognition of wasteful and haphazard processes of invention in order to keep pace with modern needs and developments, has brought about the establishment of research divisions in many of our large industries. Hundreds of carefully selected employees with special backgrounds of training and experience devote full time and effort to research and organized invention. The methods employed in research laboratories associated with large and small industries have greatly accelerated the improvement of existing products. They have brought to light innumerable new processes and useful commodities which are advantageous to industry and important to the progress and standard of living of our country.

Coupled with the research divisions supported by industry, many of our universities and land-grant colleges are carrying on similar research programs at public expense by means of contributions by private donors or by endowments. These programs in industry and in colleges will do much to maintain the position the United States has attained in serving its own citizens and the people of all the world. The fact remains that, in spite of these organized efforts in research and invention, many of the ideas which are carried to final development originate in the minds of workmen and other individuals possessing inventive ability. If knowledge of the basic sciences underlying most of our progress could be provided the workers in industry, the improvements and developments in many fields would be astonishing.

Summary. The new devices and new processes which come from research, invention, and discovery give industry its drive and incentive. These devices and processes, in turn, require for their development new tools, new appliances, new operations, and new methods to which both workers and leaders must be adapted and readapted. This continuous process of adjustment demands that new skills and new technical knowledge be transmitted to producers in widely diversified lines of work spread over the country and beyond our own boundaries. This is an accommodation for which the haphazard methods of pickup training have been found entirely inadequate.

Systematic procedures must be found to equip American producers to meet the changing demands of their crafts. These are the methods that the authors of this book believe constitute organized vocational education. As such education is effected, so will the contributions of the scientist and the inventor find their highest utilization. Greater skill and job intelligence will be developed and the sum of human knowledge will be increased.

CHAPTER III

First State System of Free Industrial Education (1906)

For almost three centuries after the first settlement at James-town, Virginia (1607), this nation failed to promote the democratiz-ing of education by laws providing free training for employment.

I. FIRST (OR DOUGLAS) COMMISSION 1905–6

At long last, the Massachusetts legislature of 1905 authorized Governor William L. Douglas to appoint a Commission to investi-gate educational needs for different grades of skill and responsibility in the various industries of the state. A statement setting forth the duty of the Commission follows:

"They shall investigate how far the needs are met by existing institutions and shall consider what new forms of educational effort may be advisable and shall make such investigations as may be practicable through printed reports and testimony of experts as to similar educational work done by other states, by the United States Government, and by foreign governments."[1]

According to the Officer of the Massachusetts Board of Educa-tion (1917), the resulting report of the Douglas Commission was "a history-making document."

Report of Douglas Commission. The Commission's investiga-tion considered both the welfare of the industries and adult work-men and the welfare of prospective young wage earners. Conclu-sions were based upon facts regarding industrial and school conditions. Recommendations were aimed at the education of youth along lines which would correct industrial situations. Resulting legislation provided opportunities for new types of free vocational training.

Findings from the public hearings held in the principal cities of the state, as briefly summarized here, were:

---

[1] *Twenty-fifth Annual Report of the U.S. Commission of Labor* (1910). Revised Laws of Massachusetts (Washington, D.C.: Government Printing Office, 1911).

1. Widespread interest in special training for vocations.

2. Lack of skilled workmen in industry—not simply a want of manual dexterity (though that was common), but of industrial intelligence.

3. Public schools, too exclusively literary in spirit, scope, and methods.

4. Suspicion and hostility on the part of some trade unions. It was feared that the Commission would formulate a plan for trade schools which would affect the labor market. Technical schools could not solve vocational school problems.

5. General feeling that the expense of the needed industrial education should be borne wholly or in part by the state.

"The wide difference of opinion regarding manual training as a school subject may be due to the narrow view which has prevailed amongst its chief advocates. It has been urged as a cultural subject mainly useful as a stimulant to other forms of intellectual effort—a sort of mustard relish; an appetizer to be conducted without reference to any industrial end. It has been severed from real life as have other school activities. Thus, it has come about that the overmastering influence of school traditions have brought into subjection both drawing and the manual work."[2]

Describing the youth situation of the time, it was stated that 25,000 Massachusetts children between 14 and 16 years of age were either at work or idle. It was estimated that one out of every six completed the grammar grades. The years from 14 to 16 were wasted since these children were neither learning a trade nor preparing for any kind of life occupation. Parents were stubbornly convinced that the school offered the child of 14 little that would serve him in his wage-earning life. If the practical advantage to youth of remaining in school had been seen, perhaps 66 per cent of those estimated at work or idle could have continued their education to the age of 16.

Conclusions of Douglas Commission. As a result of the public hearings and special investigation, the Commission arrived at the following conclusions:

1. In regard to children who leave school for employment at age 14 and/or 15, the first three or four years are practically wasted years so far as the actual productive value of the child is concerned or as far as increasing his industrial or

---

[2] *Ibid.*, pp. 504–506.

productive efficiency is concerned. Employments which they may enter are not educative in any sense.

2. These children, many of whom leave school voluntarily at the completion of the seventh grade, would find further training of a practical character attractive and a possibility if it prepared for the industries. Any educational plan to increase the child's productive efficiency must consider the child of fourteen.

3. Children who continue in any well-organized school until sixteen or eighteen, especially if they complete a high-school course, are able to enter upon employments of a higher grade, usually in mercantile pursuits. They are able, by reason of greater maturity and better mental training, to learn the technique of their employment in a shorter time. But they are wholly lacking in manual skill and in what we call industrial intelligence. For the purpose of training for efficiency in productive employments, the added years spent in school are to a considerable extent lost years.

4. This condition (the lack of agencies for training) tends to increase the cost of production, to limit the output and to lower the grade in quality. Industries recruited as in paragraph 3 cannot long compete with similar industries recruiting technically trained men. In the long run, that industry, wherever it is located, which combines general intelligence, the broadest technical knowledge, and the highest technical skill, commands the markets of the world.

5. The industries of Massachusetts need—in addition to the general intelligence furnished by the public school system and the skill gained in the narrow fields of subdivided labor—a broader training in the principles of the trades. It needs a finer culture in taste as applied to workmanship and design. Whatever may be the cost of such training, failure to furnish it would in the end be more costly.

6. The state needs a wider diffusion of industrial intelligence as a foundation for the highest technical success. This can only be acquired in connection with the general system of education into which it should enter as an integral part from the beginning.

7. The investigation has shown the increasing necessity for woman to enter the industrial world for self-support. She should be prepared to earn a living wage. The attempt should be made to fit her so that she can and will enter those industries which are most closely allied to the home.

Recommendations of Douglas Commission. The Commission did not deem it its duty, under provisions of the resolve creating it, to formulate exhaustive and specific plans for industrial education. Instead, it attempted to ascertain and exhibit the needs of such education. It tried to point out how the state may make effective its existing policy. It suggested means by which the industrial development of the state might be furthered. Respecting the growth and development of industrial education on a statewide basis, the Commission made the following three recommendations:

1. That cities and towns "so modify the work in the elementary schools as to include for boys and girls instruction and practice in the elements of productive

industry, including agriculture and the mechanic and domestic arts, and that the instruction in mathematics, the sciences, and drawing should show the application and use of these subjects in industrial life."

2. That all "towns and cities provide, by new elective industrial courses in high schools, instruction in the principles of agriculture and the domestic and mechanic arts; that, in addition to day courses, cities and towns provide evening courses for persons already employed in trades; and that provision be made for instruction in part-time day classes of children between the ages of 14 and 18 years who may be employed during the remainder of the day."

3. The Commission recognized that there should be no interference with the public school system. Yet it believed that the elements of industrial training, agriculture, domestic, and mechanical sciences, should be taught in the public schools. They also recognized that there should be, in addition to this elementary teaching, distinctive industrial schools separated entirely from the public school system. The Commission for Industrial Education would deal solely and entirely with such schools, thus abrogating the Act of 1872 (Section 10, Chapter 42, of the Revised Laws of Massachusetts). This would leave the school authorities on their own initiative to introduce new industrial courses in the public schools.

The Commission endeavored to preserve the integrity of the public school system. It tried to enrich the public school along industrial lines and to expand it along vocational lines through independent industrial schools. This seemed necessary because the current public school system was designed primarily to secure cultural and not industrial or vocational effects. The system recommended by the Commission, relative to independent industrial schools, would secure a development of the principles of efficient, industrial instruction.

II. SECOND COMMISSION ON INDUSTRIAL EDUCATION

In June, 1906, the Douglas Commission concluded its report with the recommendation that an administrative commission should be created to carry out the recommendations embodied in the report:

The Commission should be charged with the responsibility of developing and administering a state system of local public industrial schools; should be assisted with a paid officer; should carry on its work independent of the state board of education; and should be authorized to pay one-half the total cost of operation of all approved industrial schools maintained by communities independent of their regular public school system.

These recommendations were incorporated in a bill adopted by the General Court of Massachusetts and signed by Governor Douglas. For a brief period this act created a dual system of education. One was for general education under the State Board of Education and through the regular public school system of the community. Another was for industrial education under the new Commission and through local industrial schools operated by independent local boards.

Unfortunately, the new Commission was unable to agree on problems concerning the duties devolving upon it. As the demand for vocational education has been made by manufacturers representing many different industries, the Commission decided to consult their wants by interviewing 900 leading employers.

Their ideas revealed many different opinions of what needed to be done. The study not only failed to help the Commission, but added to its confusion. So little was accomplished that, in 1909, the work of the Commission was merged by the Massachusetts General Court with that of the State Board of Education. Vocational schools under the direction of the Board became "wards" of a deputy commissioner serving under the Commissioner of Education. In this way, Massachusetts returned to the unit system of state public education through one board. Yet it retained the dual system under which approved local vocational schools were operated independently of other public schools of the community.

In 1909, the State Board called Dr. David Snedden to become State Commissioner of Education. Charles A. Prosser was made State Director of Vocational Education. Charles R. Allen was made an agent for industrial education. In consequence of these changes there ensued ". . . the rapid development of a comprehensive scheme of vocational education, in connection with the public schools of Massachusetts, which served as a model for study and inspired action by other states."[3]

To express appreciation for the constructive service rendered by Dr. Snedden to vocational as well as to general education, the Board of Education, through its State Office of Education, issued a special bulletin.[4] Dr. Snedden had at that time terminated ten years of service as Commissioner of Education in the Commonwealth. The bulletin concluded with the following statement:

---

[3] Charles A. Bennett, *History of Manual and Industrial Education* (Peoria, Ill.: Chas. A. Bennett Press, Inc., 1937), Vol. II, p. 517.

[4] Bulletin No. 6 (Whole No. 65) of the Board of Education, Commonwealth of Massachusetts (1917).

The valuable pioneer labors of the Commission on Industrial Education were supplemented upon the advent of Dr. David Snedden as Commissioner of Education by his contribution of a philosophy as to the aims, scope, and extent of this new type of education.

It seems especially appropriate here to consider the conclusions and recommendations contained in the report of the Industrial Commission, to review certain accomplishments of this period, and to take a concise presentation of the statutes of state-aided vocational education at this time. Such a program affords an opportunity to evaluate the conclusions and recommendations of the Commission in the light of a decade of experience and to determine in part the degree to which the responsibility for the establishment of vocational education of secondary grade has been discharged in terms of the Commission's recommendations.

The recommendations of the Commission had called for the establishment of schools which would provide training in agriculture, domestic occupations, and industrial pursuits. They also proposed that opportunities be afforded in day, part-time, and evening schools. The Office declared for Massachusetts that all these opportunities had been provided, and that, in all of them except the part-time schools, signal success had attended the establishment of the schools and the courses.

From the recommendations of the Douglas Commission and the bill through which it proposed to create a separate state and local system of vocational schools, the U.S. Office of Education also drew these conclusions:

They show that it was the intention of the Douglas Commission to establish a new type of education. The schools established to administer it were to receive state aid for doing specific educational work of a vocational character.

These schools were not recommended as a part of the general public school system. They were not to undertake work in competition with the public schools established for giving general education. They were to be established to afford a separate and distinct opportunity for those pupils electing the special training therein offered.

As the normal schools were planned to train prospective teachers, so the vocational schools were planned to train prospective artisans, craftsmen, and homemakers for specific vocational callings. This idea was embodied in the original and supplementary legislation. The schools established have aimed to carry out this intent.

CHAPTER IV

Smith-Lever Act (1914)

Beginning in 1802, Congress received petitions for financial aid to colleges through grants of land which could be sold and the proceeds used for the support of education. Congress responded favorably by adopting a series of acts appropriating funds to the states for agricultural and mechanic arts (engineering) education through their land-grant colleges. They were so called because grants of land from Congress played such an important part in their development:

1. *First Morrill Act* (adopted, July 2, 1862). The Act was named after Senator Justin A. Morrill of Vermont. It was an original land-grant act and was designated as "An act donating public lands to the several states and territories which may provide colleges for the benefit of agriculture and the mechanic arts."

2. *Hatch Act* (adopted, 1887). This Act (also known as the Experimental Stations Act) appropriated $15,000 in money to each state to be used to establish an agricultural experiment station. This sum was later increased. Its designated purpose was ". . . to aid in acquiring and diffusing among the people of the United States useful and practical information respecting the principle and application of agricultural science."

3. *Second Morrill Act* (adopted, 1890). This Act (also known as the Maintenance Act) authorized the application of a portion of the proceeds from the sale of public lands under the first Morrill Act to the more complete endowment and support of the land-grant colleges, and for the benefit of agriculture and the mechanic arts. Each state and territory received an increase of $1,500 annually. This amount was to be supplemented by an automatic annual increase of $1,000 until the year 1900.

4. *Adams Act* (adopted, 1906). By enactment of this law the original annual appropriation of $15,000 to each state provided by the Hatch Act was increased to $30,000.

5. *Nelson Amendment* (adopted, 1907). The Amendment provided an increase of federal aid to the states for the land-grant col-

leges from grants of $25,000 per state, annually, to $35,000, with increases of $5,000 each year until $15,000 had been reached.

6. *State Marine School Act* (adopted, 1911). This Act provided training for those planning a seafaring career. Its importance to vocational education is primarily concerned with the fact that it introduced the principle of "matching" federal aid by appropriation of funds on the part of state and local governments.

7. *Agricultural Extension Act* (adopted, 1914). This Act (also called the Smith-Lever Act) provided for a program of cooperative extension work in agriculture and home economics. It stipulated that "cooperative agricultural work shall consist of the giving of instruction and practical demonstration in agriculture and home economics to persons not attending or resident in the colleges in the several communities, and imparting to such persons information on such subjects through field demonstrations, publications, and otherwise." The statute provides continuous annual appropriations to match with a federal dollar every state dollar spent for extension training.

As a history of vocational education of less than college grade, this chapter will focus its attention on the development of extension training for the "dirt farmer" rather than upon professional training in agriculture of college grade. Service to the employed farmer is just as clearly vocational training as the instruction given urban workers in part-time and evening classes.

Increase of subsidies to land-grant colleges made by previous grants followed later with passage of the Purnell Act in 1925, the Capper-Ketcham Act in 1928, and the Bankhead-Jones Act in 1935. These Acts were influenced by the provisions of the Smith-Lever and Vocational Education Acts, and by the recommendations embodied in the Report of the National Commission on Federal Aid to Vocational Education. Thus it was that a national subsidy system of free public vocational education unrivaled in all history was developed in this country.

CONTRIBUTIONS OF AGRICULTURAL EXTENSION ACT

1. *Democratizing the land-grant colleges.* Congress had been more generous to the land-grant colleges than to any other public educational institution. As a result these schools have, as a group, been better endowed and better prepared financially to meet new oppor-

tunities for service than have other educational institutions. When they wanted funds for new services or additional funds for services already existing, Congress usually granted them.

The record for 1939–40 shows that the 69 land-grant colleges had a total income of more than 165 million dollars. They expended less than 153 million dollars. The colleges ended the year with a total unexpended balance—in their dealings with their respective states—of more than 12 million dollars, an average "profit" of more than $190,000 per college.

Out of this cumulative abundance of funds not one dollar could be spent by these colleges for any purpose other than the professional training of candidates for a degree in technical subjects. When the Agricultural Extension Act was on its passage through Congress, Senator Hoke Smith, chief sponsor for the measure, pointed out very clearly the difference between the professional education these colleges were already providing and the training to be established under the Agricultural Extension Act for the farmer and his family on the home acres.

For more than half a century Congress, the states, and the land-grant colleges ignored the vital needs of this agrarian nation and its farmers. It is true, however, that the land-grant colleges had liberalized their curricula of college grade by providing professional training in new subjects for new professions in agriculture and in industry.

Meanwhile American farmers, like the neglected workmen of the cities, could, in too many cases, acquire the art and mystery of their calling only by the pickup methods of observation, imitation, guess-work, and trial and error—a costly experience for both the farmer and the nation. When the Smith-Lever Act met this situation by providing aid for needed training in demonstration and project work at the farm, it further liberalized and democratized the land-grant colleges. This was a contribution which also made it at once the most popular of all the land-grant college services to the states.

2. *The beginning of a federal subsidy system.* All the previous grants to the states for their land-grant colleges had been loosely drawn. As chief sponsor for the Smith-Lever Act, Senator Hoke Smith did a masterful job in applying the sound principles, policies, procedures, and safeguards prescribed in the Agricultural Extension Act. Along with the *Report of the National Commission on Federal Aid to*

Vocational Education (*1914*) and the Smith-Hughes Act, they constitute an enduring contribution to a federal subsidy system for all public education, general as well as vocational.

3. In the eleven years from 1914 to 1925, inclusive, the growth of agricultural extension training was so rapid that the total annual expenditures of the land-grant colleges for supervision and instruction in that service rose from $480,000 to $11,279,084 and the federal subsidy from $480,000 to $5,886,000 annually. Over the period, the total outlay of state and national moneys was $75,992,-185, of which $40,680,000 was contributed as a Government subsidy under the Smith-Lever Act. Not one cent of that contribution was lost by theft or misuse. That record—as to success and proper safeguard of grants to the states—is fully paralleled by the Smith-Hughes Act.

CHAPTER V

Congress Creates a Commission on
National Aid to Vocational Education

In every movement requiring federal legislation, Congress usually serves as an experimental laboratory. In Congress it is learned what can be done, and how it may be accomplished as well as what cannot be done, and the reason for its impossibility. Vocational education proved to be no exception.

During the forty-four-year period from 1862 to 1906, five acts were adopted by the federal government making general gifts, virtually without restriction, to land-grant colleges for professional education of college grade in agriculture and the mechanic arts. Not one cent, however, was provided for the training of American workers for the farm, the shop, or the home.

Even after the congressional election of 1913 had given the Democrats a small majority in the Senate, Senator Smith, in spite of his fine leadership, still found it difficult to secure a senate majority for the Smith-Lever Bill. He had always favored the appointment of a national commission to study the difficult problems involved in a national system of federal aid to the states for secondary education which were not encountered in the system providing aid for land-grant colleges. He was aware that the office of the National Society for the Promotion of Industrial Education also favored this plan.

A gentlemen's agreement was reached between Senator Smith and officers of the Society. The Senator promised that if the Smith-Lever Bill were adopted he would offer a resolution creating a commission to study the unsolved problems of the Page-Wilson Bill.

President Appoints a Commission. The events that followed were: adoption of the Smith-Lever Act in January, 1914, defeat on the same day of the Page-Wilson Bill in Joint Conference Committee, and the tendering of a resolution the following day by Senator Smith. The resolution was adopted unanimously by the Senate and approved by the President on January 20, 1914. That resolution authorized the President to appoint a Commission composed of nine members. It defined the duties of the Commission and set the time at which a report with recommendations was to be submitted.

It appropriated funds to meet the expenditures of the Commission, and regulated the use of the funds.

Everybody seemed satisfied—even Senator Page who, at the eleventh hour, had accepted a new version of his own bill from the office of the National Society. As a member of the Commission, he had the satisfaction later of seeing the principles and policies of that version live again in the legislation recommended by the Commission. Vocational education never had a more enthusiastic friend and advocate. While he proved no match as a resourceful parliamentary leader to Senator Hoke Smith, his integrity and devotion helped greatly to turn defeat into victory for the cause he had so earnestly served on the Commission.

Most gratifying to all concerned was the fact that in less than 60 days, the Commission had produced a two-volume report of almost 500 pages. It covered virtually every phase of the many problems involved in a comprehensive study of national aid to the states for the new education. The original report is now out of print.

The Commission on Vocational Education presented to Congress its findings and recommendations for a federally aided system of vocational education based on state aid and cooperation. These provisions were subsequently enacted into federal law by the unanimous sanction of Congress.

Many of the principles and arguments which gave both Congress and the public an understanding of the obligation to provide vocational training as a joint responsibility of both the state and the nation are outlined in Sections I and II of the *Report of the Commission on National Aid to Vocational Education.*

Sections I and II of the Commission's report served a double purpose: (1) to furnish information needed by every citizen, and (2) to win support of the Commission's recommendations.

NEED FOR VOCATIONAL EDUCATION

The Commission recognizes at the outset that the term "vocational education" is employed in current discussion to describe a wide variety of schools and training. For the purpose of this report, however, its use will be confined to that kind of practical education which the commission feels has been largely neglected up to the present time, and which most urgently needs encouragement, namely, that which prepares boys and girls for useful employment. Limiting the use of the term in its own work, the Commission disclaims all intention of attempting to define the scope of vocational education as a whole, or of restricting its meaning for ordinary usage. It is clearly recognized not only that a stronger vocational element is needed in general education, but that no vocational school is worthy the name which fails to give a considerable amount of general education along with special preparation for a vocation. The purpose of restricting the term in this report is that of securing clearness in the presentation of the findings and recommendations of the Commission.

For the reasons given, the Commission is of the opinion that the kind of vocational education which is most needed at the present time is that which is designed to prepare workers for the more common occupations in which the great mass of our people find useful employment. Vocational training, to be most effective and thoroughgoing, should be restricted to persons over 14 years of age who have laid the foundation of a general education in the elementary school. Because of the kind of workers to be reached and the character of instruction to be given, this vocational education should be of less than college grade. The states, aided in part by the National Government, have already given substantial encouragement to and offered fairly adequate opportunities for training in the professions, in the arts and sciences, and for leadership in commercial and industrial activities. What we need now is practical education of secondary grade to reach the great body of our workers.

Wherever the term "vocational education" is used in this report, it will mean, unless otherwise explained, that form of education whose controlling purpose is to give training of a secondary grade to persons over 14 years of age for increased efficiency in useful employment in the trades and industries, in agriculture, in commerce and commercial pursuits, and in callings based upon a knowledge of home economics. The occupations included under these are almost endless in number and variety. As illustrative of their general character, a few of the common pursuits may be noted.

In the *trades* and *industries:* The work of the carpenter, the mason, the baker, the stonecutter, the electrician, the plumber, the machinist, the toolmaker, the engineer, the miner, the painter, the typesetter, the linotype operator, the shoe cutter and laster, the tailor, the garment maker, the straw-hat maker, the weaver, the glove maker.

In *agriculture:* The work of general farming, orcharding, dairying, poultry raising, truck gardening, horticulture, bee culture, and stock raising.

In *commerce* and *commercial pursuits:* The work of the bookkeeper, the clerk, the stenographer, the typist, the auditor, and the accountant.

In *home economics:* The work of the dietitian, cook and housemaid, institution manager, and household decorator.

Size of the Problem. The immediate need of providing vocational education for this country is well illustrated by the size of the problem before us.

According to the census of 1910, there were 12,659,203 persons in the United States, both male and female, engaged in agriculture. While it is impossible to secure accurate figures, it is probable that less than 1 per cent of these have had adequate preparation for farming. This means that there are over 12,000,000 people engaged in agriculture in this country who are not trained to deal with the soil in such a way as to make it produce, through scientific methods, what it should yield in order to sustain the present and future life of this nation.

Engaged in manufacturing and mechanical pursuits and allied industries there were 14,261,376. It is equally correct to say that not one out of every hundred of these workers have had, or are having at the present time, any adequate chance to secure training.

The American people have hardly begun the work of providing for the practical education of these millions of our wageworkers. In this whole country there are fewer trade schools than were to be found in the little German kingdom of Bavaria, with a population not much greater than that of New York City. There were more workers being trained at public expense in the city of Munich alone than in all the larger cities of the United States, representing a population of more than 12,000,000. It is substantially true that practically every German citizen who could profit by it may receive vocational training for his life work in the schools and classes supported out of the public treasury. Since commercial prosperity depends largely upon the skill and well-being of our workers, the outlook for American commerce, in competition with that of our German neighbors, is under present conditions not very promising.

To provide in our educational system some opportunity for our workers to improve their efficiency and thereby better their own and the communities' well-being, is a social obligation which cannot be avoided with impunity. But, disregarding for the moment this obligation, even to replace the annual mortality and superannuation of our great army of workers, each year more than 1,000,000 young people are required. Simply to maintain the ranks of our working population, therefore, the immediate problem of vocational education is the problem of equipping for the successful pursuit of some useful trade or occupation the youth who go to work at the rate of more than 1,000,000 a year.

If it be assumed that three years' special training are required by each one to prepare for a calling, our vocational schools must provide for the continuous instruction of more than 3,000,000 persons, without taking into account the work which should be done in behalf of the millions more of untrained adult workers already on the farm and in the shop, or making any allowance for the growth of our population or of our industries. For this great task the facilities and resources of our public schools are entirely inadequate without the help of the larger resources of the National Government.

ECONOMIC NEED FOR VOCATIONAL EDUCATION

The two great assets of a nation which enter into the production of wealth, whether agricultural or industrial, are natural resources and human labor. The conservation and full utilization of both of these depend upon vocational training.

1. *Vocational Training Required to Conserve and Develop Our Natural Resources.* As the asset of natural resources lessens or falls in the scale, the asset of human labor rises in importance. American agriculture has prospered in the past because it rested upon the basis of the richest soil in the world—a fertility which, with the usual prodigality of this people, has been treated as if it were inexhaustible. This favorable condition itself has delayed, for a century too long in the United States, the cooperation of the National Government with the states in the systematic training of the American farmer. Only thoroughgoing agricultural education, making the farmer an intelligent user of the natural wealth with which Providence has blessed us as a people, can restore and preserve our boasted agricultural supremacy.

A virgin fertility of soil is no longer available for unintelligent exploitation over any considerable area in the United States, and, in the future, a permanent and increasingly productive and profitable agriculture can be achieved throughout the country only by scientific culture. In agriculture, science has advanced far beyond practice, and it has become essential for the welfare of our increasing population that the farmer be made an expert. For intelligent farming our soils are an inexhaustible source of wealth.

The American manufacturer has prospered in the past because of four factors:

a) The abundance and cheapness of raw material.
b) The inventive genius of this people.
c) Organizing ability leading to production on a large scale.
d) A great body of cheap foreign labor of the first generation working its way upward in our midst to civic and industrial worth.

With the opening of new sources of supply in foreign countries, and with the gradual depletion of our own virgin resources in many lines, our advantage from an abundance and cheapness of raw material, at least so far as regards commercial competition, is a decreasing one. We cannot continue to draw indefinitely on Europe for cheap labor, nor will cheap labor in the immediate future meet the urgent need in American industry for the more intelligent service necessary if we are to satisfy the rising demand for a better product from our domestic as well as our foreign markets. In the proportion that our resource factor fails must we increase the efficiency of human labor in the shop as well as on the farm.

The conservation and full utilization of our natural resources can be accomplished only in proportion as we train those who handle them. Public discussion and legislative fiat must be supplemented by an agricultural education which will teach the farmer how to make the soil yield an abundance and at the same time leave it rejuvenated; and by an industrial education which will teach our workers in shops and factories how to use material without waste, and how to turn the products of our forests and our mines into articles of higher and still higher value.

2. *Vocational Training Needed to Prevent Waste of Human Labor.* The greatest treasure which this country holds today is the undeveloped skill and vocational possibilities, not only of the millions of our workers everywhere, but of the great army of our school children, hundreds of thousands of whom pass annually from the doors of our elementary schools to serve in the shop, the field, and the office. So far we have given but little attention to the conservation of our human resources.

Vocational education will reduce to a minimum the waste of labor power, the most destructive form of extravagance of which a people can be guilty.

In any organized community, within a country, there are always to be found three basically characteristic forms of the waste labor power:

a) The army of the unemployed or the involuntary idle.
b) The imperfectly employed or the untrained.
c) The improperly employed, the acquisitively rather than the productively employed.

It is sufficiently obvious that the waste of labor by imperfect or by improper employment can be largely avoided by vocational training in the elements of useful crafts. Such training is, moreover, the most certain remedy for unemployment. As bearing upon this point and upon the general advantage of vocational training, the following statement[1] may be quoted:

"If by means of training you can transfer unskilled labor into the scarcer and more needed work of management, you provide a demand for the army of unemployed and increase the productive power of the community. Upon the distribution of labor power upward from the unskilled and overcrowded occupations toward and into remunerative occupations depends more than anything else the expansion of our industries. It takes no miracle to see it; it requires only education."

3. *Vocational Training Needed to Provide a Supplement to Apprenticeship.* The American industrial worker, with all his native qualities, is, relatively speaking, becoming more unskilled. Since the schools have as yet assumed no responsibility for those who go to work, the youth must get the rest of his education in an industrial organization, which no longer is able or willing to train its own workers. Large-scale production, extreme division of labor, and the all-conquering march of the machine, have practically driven out the apprenticeship system through which, in a simpler age, young helpers were taught not simply the technique of some single process, but the "arts and mysteries of a craft." The journeyman and artisan have given way to an army of machine workers, performing over and over one small process at one machine. They turn out one small part of the finished article, and know nothing about the business beyond their narrow and limited task. The age of science and invention has brought in its wake a great body of knowledge, related to the work of the mechanic and necessary to his highest success, which the shop cannot give without the help of the schools.

In the skilled callings the young worker seldom gets the breadth of experience or the information which he must have in order to realize himself, and he must, under present conditions, remain on a relatively low level of skill. Most of those who leave school at the age of 14, finding the doors of the skilled occupations closed to them, tend to enter all sorts of low-grade skilled and unskilled industries, affording little or no opportunity for better wages or for promotion to a desirable life work. In the absence of a system of education which will follow them to these tasks and by continued training show them a way to efficiency and happiness, makes the time which most of these children spend in the factory unprofitable, both to themselves and to society. The few adolescents who rise to success as wage earners, whether by accident, rule of thumb, or sheer force of native qualities, acquire their skill and insight in ways that are wasteful to them and to business.

4. *Vocational Training Needed to Increase Wage-Earning Power.* The practical training of workmen in any pursuit brings both immediate and lasting economic returns in increased production and wage-earning capacity. The returns of our older trade, technical, and apprenticeship schools show that the wage-earning power of their graduates increases as a direct result of training. For the thoroughly trained worker, wages advance from year to year with age and increased capacity with no fixed limit. While the average increase is large, individual increase is also very large.

---

[1] Prof. Arthur Henry Carver, as quoted in Edwin G. Cooley, *Vocational Education in Europe*, a report to the Commercial Club of Chicago (1912), p. 28.

5. *Vocational Training Needed to Meet Increasing Demand for Trained Workmen.* With the constantly increasing demand upon industries for more and better goods, the supply of trained workers is diminishing. We are beginning to feel the inevitable economic results of a relatively low output, increased cost of production, and stationary or diminishing wages as measured by their purchasing power. The products of our factories are being restricted in quantity and quality. High prices are due in part to inefficient labor, and low profits to the same cause. Inaction means promotion of poverty and low standards of living and a general backwardness in industry.

6. *Vocational Training Needed to Offset Increased Cost of Living.* With a farming area practically stationary, an increasing population, and an agricultural class whose ability with present methods to meet demands for larger production is relatively diminishing, our national appetite has outgrown both our national larder and national pocketbook. Population tends to press upon subsistence. The cost of the necessaries of life has risen faster than the earning power of the consumer and has operated to reduce the actual income of the wageworker and make the struggle for existence hard, not only to the common laborer but even to the trade worker of small means. For millions of our people life has, as a result, been narrowed and sombered.

7. *Vocational Education a Wise Business Investment.* Expenditures for vocational education are wise business investments which will yield large returns, not only in educational and social betterment but in money itself, than a similar sum spent for other purposes. The commission recognizes that boys and girls cannot be valued in terms of dollars and cents, save as these represent returns in social well-being both to themselves and society. The financial argument shown is offered from that standpoint alone.

More than 25,000,000 persons over 18 in this country are engaged in farming, mining, manufacturing, and mechanical pursuits, trade and transportation.[2]

If we assume that a system of vocational education, pursued through the years of the past, would have increased the wage-earning capacity of each of these to the extent of 10 cents a day, this would make an increase in wages for the group of $2,500,000 a day, or $750,000,000 a year, with all that this would mean to the wealth and life of the nation. This is a very modest estimate, and, while no complete figures are available, it is probably much nearer 25 cents a day, which would make a total increase in wages of $6,250,000 per day and $1,875,000,000 per year.

In 1910 there were in the United States 7,220,298 children between the ages of 14 and 18 years. It has been estimated that the total cost of bringing a child from birth to the age of 18 represents an outlay of $4,000. This is about $220 per year and includes approximately $60 per year coming not from the parents, but contributed by the state and nation. At present this great body of more than 7,000,000 youths represents on the whole an untrained army needing vocational education to make it efficient. If we assume that it would require on the average an

[2] The total engaged in agriculture, mining, manufacturing and mechanical pursuits, trade and transportation in 1910 was 30,535,249. The number in these pursuits today probably exceeds 34,000,000. Assuming the same distribution by age for these persons as is found in the total population 10 years of age and over, the number 18 years of age and over exceeds 27,000,000. The proportion under 18 years is certainly less for those gainfully employed than it is for the total population 10 years of age and over.

outlay of an additional $150 per person to prepare them for usefulness so that society might realize more fully upon their vocational and civic possibilities, certainly no businessman would hesitate a moment to expend that amount in order to make his investment of $4,000 secure and remunerative. It is even more shortsighted for the state and the nation to neglect these investments, since national success is dependent not alone on returns in dollars and cents but in civic and social well-being.

Let us assume further that the expectancy of life ahead of these youths at 18 is only thirty years. An increase of 10 cents a day in wage-earning capacity would, on this assumption, amount to $30 a year, or $900 in thirty years, in additional wages. An outlay of $150 in training between 14 and 18 years of age would thus be made to yield a return six times as great. In five years the increase in wages would cover the total cost of vocational training for each worker. If the increase in wage-earning capacity was 25 cents a day, the increase in the wage return in one year would be $75 and in thirty years $2,350, an amount fifteen times as great as the original outlay. On this assumption the increased wage-earning power could repay the cost of instruction for each worker in two years.

8. *National Prosperity at Stake.* We have become a great industrial as well as a great agricultural nation. Each year shows a smaller percentage of our people on the farms and a greater percentage in the cities.[3]

Our factory population is growing apace. Our future as a nation will depend more and more on the success of our industrial life, as well as upon the volume and quality of our agricultural products. It has repeatedly been pointed out that the time is not far distant when our rapidly increasing population will press hard upon an improved agriculture for its food supply, and force our industries to reach out over the entire world for trade wherewith to meet the demands for labor of untold millions of breadwinners.[4]

In volume of output the United States leads the four great manufacturing nations of the world. More than a billion and a half people outside these four countries are largely dependent upon them for manufactured articles. "The rewards offered in world trade are beyond comprehension. They are to be measured in money, in intellectual advancement, in national spirit, in heightened civilization."[5] Yet we have only begun to invade this market, where we find our competitor too often in possession of the field and strongly entrenched against us.

It is true that we have a large foreign trade in manufactured articles, but of our exports a very large proportion consists of crude materials. German, French,

[3] The number and percentage urban and rural in the total population of the United States is shown in the following table for the last four censuses.

Census	Urban Population	Rural Population	Percentage Urban	Rural
1880	14,772,438	35,383,345	29.5	70.5
1890	22,720,223	40,227,491	36.1	63.9
1900	30,797,185	45,197,390	40.5	59.5
1910	42,623,383	39,389,883	46.3	53.7

[4] In 1880 foodstuffs constituted 56 per cent of our total exports, in 1912 only 19 per cent. In 1880 manufactured articles made up only 15 per cent of our total exports, in 1912, 47 per cent.

[5] *Report of the Committee on Industrial Education* (National Manufacturers Association, 1912).

and English exports represent on the average a much greater value in skill and workmanship than do those from our own parts. Less than one-third of the volume of our foreign commerce is made up of manufactures ready for consumption. A very large proportion consists of raw and semi-raw materials such as lumber, cotton, meat, coal, oil, and copper bar. To secure these we have robbed our soil and the earth beneath our feet of the riches we have been foolish enough to regard as inexhaustible. The statistics of our foreign commerce show that the proportion of these raw products, in the total volume of our exports, has been declining during the past three decades and that the maintenance and development of our foreign trade is coming to depend each year to a greater extent upon our ability to compete with foreign nations in the products of skilled labor—upon our ability to "sell more brains and less material."

The volume of our foreign trade has in the past depended upon the exploitation of a virgin soil and of our other national resources. In this crude work we have had no competitors. Our profit has been the profit of the miner working in a rich soil. The volume and profitableness of our trade in the future, however, must depend much more largely upon the relative skill and efficiency of the vocationally trained artisans of England, France, and Germany. Our products will find a market in foreign countries only in those lines of industrial activity in which the labor is as efficient and as well trained as the labor of the countries with which we must compete.

The battles of the future between nations will be fought in the markets of the world. That nation will triumph, with all that its success means to the happiness and welfare of its citizenship, which is able to put the greatest amount of skill and brains into what it produces. Our foreign commerce, and to some extent our domestic commerce, are being threatened by the commercial prestige which Germany has won, largely as the result of a policy of training its workers begun by the far-seeing Bismarck almost half a century ago.

France and England, and even far-off Japan, profiting by the schools of the Fatherland, are now establishing national systems of vocational education. In Germany, within the next few years, there will probably be no such thing as an untrained man.[6] In the United States probably not more than 25,000 of the eleven or twelve million workers in manufacturing and mechanical pursuits have had an opportunity to acquire an adequate training for their work in life.

SOCIAL AND EDUCATIONAL NEED FOR VOCATIONAL TRAINING

1. Vocational Training Needed to Democratize Education.

a) By recognizing different tastes and abilities and by giving an equal opportunity to all to prepare for their life work. Equality of opportunity in our present system of education is not afforded to the mass of our children. While our schools are opened freely to every child, their aims and purposes are such that a majority of the children are unable to take advantage of them beyond a certain grade and hence do not secure at public expense a preparation for their work in life. Although here and there we see the beginnings of change, it is still true that the schools are largely planned for

---

[6] *Report of the Committee on Industrial Education* (National Manufacturers Association, 1912).

the few who prepare for college rather than for the large number who go into industry.

Only half of the children who enter the city elementary schools of the country remain to the final elementary grade, and only 1 in 10 reaches the final year of high school.[7] On the average, 10 per cent of the children have left school at 13 years of age; 40 per cent have left by the time they are 14; 70 per cent by the time they are 15; and 85 per cent by the time they are 16 years of age. On the average the schools carry their pupils as far as the fifth grade, but in some cities great numbers leave below that grade.

If we assume that all children should have a minimum school training equivalent to the eight grades of the elementary school, we must acknowledge that the schools now furnish this minimum to less than half the children who enter them. The rest leave school with inadequate general education and with no special training to fit them for work. Vocational courses are therefore needed to attract and hold in school pupils who now leave because they are unable to obtain suitable preparation for useful employment. For such pupils the vocational courses also offer the only opportunity the schools have to give further training in citizenship.

Our whole scheme of education presupposes leisure to acquire academic culture or to prepare for leadership in the professions. Vocational culture and training for leadership in industry is equally important, and these can come only when education is broadened to meet the needs of all the children; so that each and every one may have a chance to develop in accordance with his or her capacity and be prepared to render to society the particular service of which he or she is capable.

b) By extending education through part-time and evening instruction to those who must go to work in the shop or on the farm. Only a meager percentage of the workers of today are trained for their work, and the armies of children going out from school at 14 and 15 years of age annually swell the ranks of the untrained. Whether from necessity or not, the economic fact is that the mass of children go to work as soon as the laws of the various states permit. It is not solely because the children and their parents do not appreciate the value of an education that more than half of the entire number who enter the elementary school do not remain to complete it. It is, at least to some extent, because neither they nor their parents are able to see in the schools of today an opportunity for education and training to fit for callings which they must pursue. It is for the states and the nation, not only to see that these children are prepared for life's battles before they leave school, but to supplement their work by the largest possible opportunity for development in everything that makes for useful and happy citizenship.

The United States is one of the few large nations which does not provide by legislation for the continued education of children who become wage earners at 14 years of age. The period from 14 to 18 years of age is the one in which the youth is finding himself in society and setting up standards which will largely determine his future conduct and career, and it is therefore important to continue his training both for general civic intelligence and for vocational preparation. If allowed to drift during this period, or if placed in an unwholesome or degrading environment, he may fail to realize his own possibilities of development and may become a

---

[7] Leonard P. Ayres, *Laggards in Our Schools* (New York: Russell Sage Foundation, Charities Publication Committee, 1909).

dependent or injurious member of society. The adolescent period is, therefore, the critical period during which the individual wage earner needs training for citizenship as well as training for work.

2. Vocational Training Needed for Its Indirect but Positive Affect on Aims of General Education.

a) By developing a teaching process through which children who do not respond to book instruction alone may be reached and educated through learning by doing. There are many overage children in the grades, many who fail to be promoted from year to year and soon lose interest and drop out of school. Many of these retarded children are present in the few elementary vocational schools already established in this country, and many teachers in these schools have testified to the remarkable progress made by these chidren under a kind of instruction which is suited to their interests and abilites, which utilizes the experience of the child and relates the instruction to his motor activities. This is the most successful way of teaching the normal child or man.

At the same time it should be pointed out that so far as vocational schools themselves are concerned, they are by no means institutions for the primary purpose of dealing with slow or retarded children. These schools are such as to call for the best efforts of study of vigorous and intelligent boys and girls seeking preparation for an important life work.

b) By introducing into our educational system the aim of utility to take its place in dignity by the side of culture, and to connect education with life by making it purposeful and useful. The mission of vocational education is not only to provide definite training in the technique of the various occupations, but to relate that training closely to science, mathematics, history, geography, and literature which are useful to the man and woman as a worker and a citizen. Under such instruction the student worker becomes familiar with the laws of health and with his rights and obligations as a worker and a citizen in relation to his employer, his fellow employees, his family, the community, the state, and the nation. By thus relating education closely to the world's experience, it becomes purposeful and useful and enables the worker to see the significance of, to use, and to interpret in terms of his own experience, the knowledge and culture which the race has accumulated. Such education is at least entitled to a place in dignity by the side of the more formal and literary culture now given by the schools.

3. Industrial and Social Unrest Due to Lack of Vocational Training.

The absence of opportunity for creative work and, hence, for full self-expression, is without doubt, one of the causes of much of the present unrest. The tendency of large-scale production to subdivide labor almost indefinitely and to confine a worker to one monotonous process, requiring little save purely manipulative skill, while effective so far as the material product is concerned, is serious when measured in terms of human values. It is safe to say that industry in its highly organized form, with its intense specialization, is in the main narrowing to the individual worker, and while "hands" alone may satisfy the immediate demands of industry, the failure to recognize and provide for human progress and development is producing a restless and discontented people.

Out of this unrest comes a demand for a more practical education for those who toil, an education that will better fit them to progress in industry and enable them to rise to ranks of leadership and responsibility. Everywhere it is the opinion of those who are studying the conditions of society that the lack of practical education is one of the primary causes of social and industrial discontent.

Evidence presented by bureaus which are struggling with the problem of unemployment emphasizes this need. One of these bureaus[8] states that less than three out of fifty men who apply for work have had any sort of trade training or apprenticeship. Most of them have been forced to fit into some particular niche of industry as young untrained boys, have been too readily thrown out with the introduction of new inventions or devices, and thus help to swell the army of the unemployed. A former state pardon attorney has said that "nearly three-fourths of the persons found in our penitentiaries are unable to earn a living except at the most rudimentary form of labor."[9]

4. Higher Standards of Living Are Direct Result of Better Education.

Better standards of living are dependent upon two important factors, an increased earning capacity for the great mass of our people and a better understanding of values. Vocational education aims at both. Where there is intense poverty there is little hope of developing higher standards. The one hope of increasing the family income lies in better vocational training.

It is equally true that vocational education enlarges the worker's vision and arouses within him a desire for progress. This is shown by the number of men and women who, by means of further training and education, raise themselves from the ranks of unskilled labor to take positions requiring large directive powers and responsibilities. Our only hope of progress is in helping the individual to help himself. This is at the bottom of all social uplift. To educate boys and girls to perform their chosen tasks better; to understand the relation of their particular work to the whole; to know what their labor is worth and demand a proper return for it, and to broaden their horizon so that both their money and their leisure time may be spent for the things that are most worth while—this is the task of vocational education.

PUBLIC SENTIMENT FOR VOCATIONAL EDUCATION

The testimony in behalf of practical education, comes from every class of citizenship—from the educator, the manufacturer, the trades unionist, the businessman, the social worker, and the philanthropist.

In answer to the question as to whether there was need for vocational education in the various States, the 44 state superintendents of public institutions who replied all answered in the affirmative. Out of 395 city and town superintendents replying to this question, 369 declared that there was urgent need for a system of practical education for the wageworkers of their respective communities. Fourteen of the twenty-five national labor organizations replying to this question said that

---

[8] Wisconsin Employment Bureau.

[9] Statement of Mr. Speed Mosby, Missouri State pardon attorney, as quoted in an address by Mr. James W. Van Cleave before the National Society for the Promotion of Industrial Education at Chicago (1908).

the wage earners whom they represented were in favor of a system of industrial education in this country. Twenty-seven of the thirty-seven manufacturers who replied, representing skilled, semiskilled, and unskilled industries, selected by various national organizations to answer the question, said there was a great demand for the systematic training of workers for the business in which they were engaged.

At previous hearings before various committees of Congress, national organizations representing millions of people, appeared to urge upon their representatives the advisability of national grants for various forms of vocational education. During the hearings held by the Commission in the preparation of this report, some of these organizations either sent representatives to urge again the need of practical education in the United States or sent communications to the same effect.

It will not be possible in this brief report either to collect or to give any considerable space to the great number of favorable resolutions which have been passed by national, state and local organizations throughout the country. These come from societies which represent almost every phase and interest of educational, social, business, agricultural, and industrial life. A few of the most representative of these favorable declarations for vocational education are given in the Appendix, together with a list of other organizations which have passed similar resolutions.

The movement for vocational education in this country, although of slow growth during the past ten years, has already gained promising impetus and a few of the states have passed legislation. At least ten states have provided officially for commissions of one kind or another to investigate the problem of vocational education, all of whom have declared strongly in its favor, have recognized the imperative demand for it, and have recommended legislation of one kind or another for it.[10]

While, as a result of these investigations, a number of states have made commendable beginnings in vocational education of one kind or another, the progress made has been slow. This is due both to a lack of funds necessary to initiate this new form of education while continuing the regular education, and also because of the lack of prestige for vocational education, such as would be gained by national grants.

In 1910 the Royal Commission appointed by the Parliament of the Dominion of Canada began investigations of the need for vocational education in that country. The Commission has recently issued its report which indicates an overwhelming sentiment throughout the Dominion of the Provinces for its encouragement. It should be noted in passing that the similar economic conditions existing between this country and our great northern rival make the findings of the Canadian Commission most significant.

One of the strongest indications of the great demand for practical instruction in this country is shown by the eagerness with which opportunities to secure it,

---

[10] The universal opinion of these commissions, as expressed in their reports, is given in one of the findings of the Indiana Commission: Investigations of the Commission disclosed that people are not only ready but anxious for the enlargement of school work so as to include the best possible preparation for life work for all people, whether they earn their living with their heads or hands. Farmers, employees, employers, labor leaders, educators, and social workers who appeared before the Commission advocated strongly that definite, wholehearted plans be made.

even at private expense, are grasped by great numbers of students. The United States Department of Agriculture reports that registration in short courses and schools for farmers at the agricultural and mechanical colleges for 1913 was 40,416.

Even more significant are the figures which show the extent to which correspondence school instruction is being given. There are in the United States a large number of correspondence schools, the great majority of whose students are employed in wage-earning pursuits and pay their hard-earned money to secure additional training. It has been impossible to secure for this report all the facts regarding these correspondence schools, because they are private organizations and seldom publish information as to the number of their students or the extent of their business. One of the largest of these schools has, during the past 22 years, enrolled 1,651,765 pupils in the United States and Canada and is enrolling new students at the rate of 100,000 a year, most of whom come from the United States.

With the exception of a few part-time and evening schools, the total number of whose students probably is not more than 25,000 for the entire country, there are no opportunities for ambitious workers to secure instruction by direct contact with the teacher in the schoolroom. The exceptional workman undoubtedly profits by correspondence school instruction, but would profit more by schoolroom teaching. The average workman neither takes advantage of, nor could he profit much by, correspondence school instruction. Whenever, on the other hand, part-time or evening schools are established, many of these workers do attend and receive large benefits.

Just as the Smith-Lever Act is designed to meet the vocational needs of the farmer who has already gone to work on the soil, so part-time and evening schools must be established for the purpose of meeting the demands of the wage earner in the shop and in the factory. A national statute giving grants for this purpose as at least one of its provisions is the necessary complement of the Smith-Lever Act, both of which are important at this time in order that this nation may safeguard its future prosperity by the further education of its two great productive factors—the industrial worker and the farmer.

Opinions of State Superintendents of Public Instruction

Illuminating indeed are the reasons given by various state superintendents of public instruction in expressing the need for vocational education in their respective states.

"The state should point the education of every child leaving its school system, at whatever age he may leave or whatever grade he may be in at the time, with the practical education that will fit him into something in the outside world."

"No education tends to function that is not secured with a definite aim upon the part of the child as to the future application he will make of it."

"Vocational education tends to strengthen the link between the school, the home, and the after-school life."

"They develop the natural products of our state and give our youth an opportunity to become experts along these lines."

"We need vocational education because of our geographical position and resources."

"Eighty per cent of the population follow this business."

"To hitch up the schools with life."

"There is special need for trade and industrial education and almost no provisions are made by local communities for this form of instruction."

"Agriculture is one of our chief sources of productive wealth, and as an occupation needs special encouragement from us."

"Help is needed for those who must work at 15 and 16 years of age."

"Efficient preparation for trades, industry, commerce, agriculture, and household arts is a state responsibility."

"We believe in preparing the people for practical life and to make them self-sustaining."

"We need vocational education because skilled workers are needed in large numbers."

"Eighty per cent of our people live on the farm."

"Girls should be prepared to do the work at the home in the most approved fashion."

"Trained high-school students make efficient business men and women."

STATES NEED NATIONAL GRANTS FOR VOCATIONAL EDUCATION

That national grants for vocational education are necessary for its immediate and proper development, was the almost unanimous opinion of those whom the commission interrogated through its questionnaires. Only one out of the 44 state superintendents said that national aid was unnecessary. Out of 99 answers returned by county superintendents, 88 expressed the opinion that national grants were necessary to help the rural sections to develop agricultural education. Out of 375 superintendents, representing cities and towns of over 10,000 population, 320 said that national grants were necessary to help their communities bear the burden of providing industrial training for the great mass of wageworkers. Out of 57 national labor organizations, 45 said that they favored federal aid to the states for vocational education. Out of 37 manufacturers, selected by the national organizations who replied to the question, 29 said that in their opinion national grants were greatly needed to bring about the rapid development of a system of practical education in the states. These manufacturers represented various types of skilled, semiskilled, and unskilled industries.

Many great national organizations, representing every phase of educational, industrial, agricultural, civic, and social points of view, have repeatedly gone on record in favor of stimulating the states to give vocational education.

Widely varying reasons expressing the need of national grants to the states for vocational education are given in the following replies of state superintendents of public instruction to a questionnaire submitted by the Commission:

"Vocational education is not only a local function, but also a national function. This is due to the fact that the American people wander from state to state, so that state lines are tending to become less and less distinct."

"This state needs national grants for education in mining, agriculture, and household arts."

"Vocational education is needed because of the preponderance of the farming class in this state and the difficulty always attached to furnishing education of all kinds to the thinly populated rural sections."

"This is a young and rapidly growing state whose taxes are high. We need this help to fit children for efficient citizenship."

"We need help to secure properly trained teachers, directors, and superintendents. We must have men at the heads of these schools capable of doing the work which must be done to make it efficient and economical. At present such men are hard to find. We cannot pay them or hold them when we do find them."

"Certain investigations must be made to put the vocational work on a sound and economic basis. It should be worked out, not as a community, or even as a state problem, but as a national problem. This need cannot be fully met by local communities or even by states. People want immediate results and there is no time or money available for us to work out the problem that needs to be solved to place the work on a scientific and businesslike basis. The services of experts are needed to work out such problems as the following:

1. The training of vocational teachers.

2. The studying of the various occupations and industries for which we expect to prepare, with a view to determining the kind of instruction which is needed for efficient training in that field, i.e., how that trade can best be learned; what must be learned, etc.

3. The working out of the practical phase of the problem of vocational and educational guidance, as related to the problem of vocational education and the establishment of vocational schools."

"Vocational education, as at present contemplated, is peculiarly a national problem. It is beneficial to the entire community since it has to do with the happiness and productive powers of the producers in the country. Nothing is of more vital importance to the community than to serve the full talents and capacities of its future citizens. This, vocational education seeks to do. The problem is so extensive that it cannot properly be worked out unless taken up by the nation as a whole. It should also be pointed out that such a problem as vocational education will never be enthusiastically and fundamentally taken up by local communities, because school workers rarely stay in the community where they are educated. They go to other communities and states to find a better market for their labor and skill. The problem should not only be made a national one, but should be undertaken in a way that would give permanent results."

"A national appropriation could be used to good advantage if turned over to the State Board of Education and employed by that body as a stimulus to induce country communities to undertake the practical work which would equip their boys and girls to work successfully and to make and manage their homes properly."

"In all cities and towns we are voting the constitutional limit for school purposes and cannot make our schools as efficient as we want them. In most cases the towns are absolutely unable to give any vocational training in the schools."

"National grants are necessary in order that the rising generation in this state may be better equipped to cope with present-day conditions."

"National grants would extend opportunities to young men and women who prepare themselves for industrial and household arts work. There is much need for an extension of such opportunities. Such education is expensive, but confers a benefit upon the entire nation."

"This state would welcome aid from the National Government so that the industrial branches might be taught more effectively in the schools of the state."

"This state needs national grants to stimulate an interest; to direct that interest to aid in doing that which it cannot well do for itself; to contribute to the development of the country."

"It is expensive to properly inaugurate work of this kind. Our state is largely rural, and rural communities can hardly support schools where the bare essentials are taught. The cities' resources are exceeded in lengthening the time and enlarging the curriculum. The National Government must carry part of the load if trades, industries, commercial courses, and agriculture are to be taught well."

A summary of the reasons justifying national grants to the states, as given above, includes the following points:

1. To make the work of vocational training possible in those states and localities already burdened with the task of meeting the requirements for general education.

2. To help the states, with their widely varying resources, bear the burden of giving vocational education as a national service.

3. To equalize among the states the task of preparing workers, whose tendency to move from place to place is increasing, making their training for a life work a national as well as a state duty and problem.

4. To secure national assistance in solving a problem too large to be worked out extensively and permanently, except by the whole nation.

5. To give interest and prestige in the states to the work which prepares our youth for useful and productive service.

6. To secure expert information from the agencies of the National Government, bringing to bear a countrywide knowledge and viewpoint which will put the work of the states on a scientific and businesslike basis.

Urgent Need Justifies National Grants. As already pointed out, our rich asset of national resources is not being fully utilized, and our still richer asset of human labor is being constantly and rapidly wasted. Delay in dealing with the question will be disastrous. Now is the time to begin this work actively if we are to get "the right answer" to our problem. Germany, with national cooperation and aid, has 30 years the start of us in preparing her workers. Even with the help of the National Government, at least the same amount of time will be required for the states to get where the Germans are today. While the need is acute, all of the vocational training for the actual worker now being carried on in this country, though promising as an experiment, is as nothing compared with the magnitude of the task confronting us. Only eight out of the 48 states have established state systems for vocational education, and these systems are not as yet reaching even one per cent of the workers who need training.

While the task confronting us is difficult and stupendous, it can be overcome and will be overcome just in proportion as we work at it. Germany has done much, but her experience has for us only suggestion, never precedent and rule. By beginning now, under the stimulus of national encouragement, we shall learn by experiment and study how to meet the varied and complex demands of industry, due to peculiar social, economic, industrial, educational, and administrative conditions in each state and locality.

States Cannot Do the Work by Themselves. Without the aid of national grants, extensive vocational education might come in time, but very slowly. After ten years of agitation, many states have not even made beginnings in this direction.

Every commonwealth is heavily burdened with the task of meeting the new demands in general education which the twentieth century is thrusting upon the school. Restricted mainly to the revenue from a property tax, the states lack the means to cope with the task successfully. They are reluctant to tax themselves for the entire support of expensive forms of practical instruction when they see the trained men and women drifting away to other states and carrying to them rich assets in citizenship and workmanship.

Additional sources of revenue which otherwise would lie open for use by the states are being rapidly taken over by the National Government through such legislation as the income tax and the corporation tax. There are not wanting those who point out the necessity for the National Government to supplement the more limited resources of the taxing power of the states, particularly under the conditions just described, by grants for special purposes, such as vocational education.

Local communities all over the land are under a restricted taxing power, on the one hand, and, on the other, under increasing requirements, many of which have been imposed upon them by the state constitutions and laws. As a result, most of them are finding it very difficult to meet their present financial problems. The burden is particularly heavy in the communities that most need agricultural and industrial education—the small country town—and the industrial center where the demands on the taxpayer are increasing. Practical education, when given properly, will be costly as compared with regular education. To give it otherwise is a waste of time and money. Cities and towns and the country places must have aid else they will not attempt the task at all or will do it so poorly, because of their excessive burdens, that it may result in more harm than good.

Grants Justified. National grants are justified by the *interstate character* of the problem of vocational education, due to the interstate character of our industries and the national character of state business and industrial life. Because of its extreme mobility, labor, particularly that which is skilled and is therefore in great demand, has taken on a national character. A man may be born in Indiana, trained as a worker in Massachusetts, and spend his days as a machinist in California. A state cannot be expected to devote large sums from her public revenues to the making of good workmen for the benefit of other states. Only out of a common fund like the National Treasury can the burden be equalized and adjusted so that each state may, in justice, be expected to meet the obligation resting upon its schools.

Industries are so interrelated that every state is interested commercially in the quality of workmanship in every other state. Cotton is grown in Georgia, woven into cloth in Rhode Island, and consumed in Iowa. Iron is rolled in Pennsylvania or Alabama, made into plows in Wisconsin, and used in Oregon. The widespread distribution of many large-scale industries is such that state lines must be disregarded when we think of the places and problems involved, not only in the making and selling of products, but also in the education and employment of labor. A great construction company anywhere today may not only gather its working force, representing many different trades, from anywhere in the Union, but may, in the ordinary course of a year's business, send them into a dozen states.

Although we are a group of sovereign states, each one of whose constitutional rights must be carefully safeguarded, industry, commerce, and labor are so inter-related that the National Government must be the unifying agency through which the states operate. This is recognized as essential in handling all such problems as those relating to national defense, the improvement of rivers and harbors, the postal services, and the making of good roads, whose character is such that they cannot be handled properly by individual states alone. This has always been the work of the National Government, for which it was established by the Constitution. The proposal that the nation should undertake to help the states deal with the task of providing vocational training for its millions of workers is only an attempt to extend the same policy to another important endeavor which is interstate in character and is not in any way an attempt to infringe upon the right of a state to control its own educational system.

National grants for vocational education are justified by the *national character* of the problem, for it concerns all the people and is of nationwide interest and importance. It is the duty of the National Government, insofar as it does not interfere with the constitutional rights of the states, to "promote the general welfare." National efficiency is the sum total of efficiency of all individual citizens, and the national wealth is the sum of their wealth-producing capacity. While, therefore, our national prosperity in the past has been based largely upon the exploitation of our national resources, in the future it must be based more and more upon the development, through vocational education, of our national resource of human labor. In the markets of the world we compete, not as individuals, but as a unit against other nations as units. This makes the protection of our raw material and of our productive skill and human labor a national problem, and unquestionably introduces a national element into vocational education, making the right preparation of the farmer and the mechanic of vital concern to the nation as a whole. On national grounds, therefore, federal aid for vocational education becomes necessary and unless it is undertaken as a national duty, the national welfare, which is a time-honored provision of the Constitution, is at stake.

National Grants Justified by Abundant Precedent. Since the founding of the Government, Congress has passed in all more than forty-two acts which conferred directly upon all the states, or upon specific states, usually at the time of their admission to the Union, national grants of either land or money to be expended for the benefit of education. The amount and character of these grants, as given in Monroe's *Cyclopedia of Education*, are as follows, the figures given being in a number of cases "not exactly accurate, but rather, the nearest possible approximation."[11] (Table indicating Federal Grants may be found on page 44.)

Grants for Higher Forms of Vocational Education. President Lincoln signed in 1862 the Morrill Act, which granted to the states tracts of land having a total area half as large as Indiana. It inaugurated the policy of federal aid for vocational education of college grade to prepare young men for leadership in agriculture and all the mechanic arts. In the wake of this measure which founded the agricultural and mechanical colleges has come a series of congressional acts appropriating annual sums of money. In 1887 additional grants were given to these colleges which

[11] Monroe, *op. cit.*

brought about a new departure in the matter of government aid. The Hatch Act provides a direct appropriation of $15,000 per year from the proceeds of the sale of public lands to each state for the maintenance of an agricultural experiment station, to conduct researches or experiments bearing directly upon agriculture. Subsequently this grant was increased to $30,000 a year. Under these acts more than $15,000,000 has been paid directly to the states for experimental work in agriculture.[12]

AMOUNTS AND PURPOSES OF FEDERAL GRANTS

Grant and Purpose	Acres Granted	Fund Derived from Sales	Probable Future Income*	Total Income
For Common Schools:				
Sections for Schools	81,064,300	$103,000,000	$410,000,000	$513,000,000
Saline Grants	900,000	1,000,000	. . . .	1,000,000
5% of Land Sales	. . . .	7,187,316	7,000,000	14,000,000
Surplus Revenue	. . . .	14,000,000	. . . .	14,000,000
Internal Improvement Act	5,000,000	6,000,000	8,000,000	14,000,000
Swampland Grants	45,000,000	15,000,000	2,000,000	17,000,000
Forest Reserve Per Cent	. . . .	1,000,000	*25,000,000	26,000,000
Totals	131,964,300	147,187,316	452,000,000	599,000,000
Aid for Higher Education:				
University Grants	3,407,643	5,000,000	27,500,000	32,500,000
Land Grant Colleges:				
Grants of Land	11,367,832	13,736,178	25,000,000	39,000,000
Experiment Station Grants	. . . .	14,000,000	*30,000,000	44,000,000
Laws 1890 and 1907	. . . .	23,920,000	*62,500,000	86,420,000
Totals	14,775,475	56,656,178	145,000,000	†201,920,000
Grants for Other Types of Schools:				
Normal Schools	1,500,000	2,500,000	17,500,000	20,000,000
Deaf, Dumb, and Blind	560,000	. . . .	5,600,000	5,600,000
Reform Schools	500,000	. . . .	5,000,000	5,000,000
Totals	2,560,000	$2,500,000	$28,100,000	$†30,600,000
Summary of Grants	149,299,775	206,343,494	725,100,000	831,520,000

* Calculated for 20 years from 1911 at present rate of increase.
† These totals are not the correct sums of the items, but are given as shown in the work cited.

The results under the grant proved so beneficial that in 1890 the Nelson Act was passed, providing a direct annual grant to each state for maintenance and for the further support of the agricultural colleges. Beginning with $15,000 a year to

[12] Unless some other source is indicated, the data relating to national grants given in this and the following sections are taken principally from Monroe's *Cyclopedia of Education*, articles: "National Government of the United States and Education" and "Agricultural Education."

each state, this annual appropriation has been increased until the Act of 1907 granted $50,000 a year to each state, involving with the $30,000 for experimental work a total annual cash appropriation of $4,000,000 for the fifty states and territories which are eligible. The total cash grants to the agricultural and mechanical colleges, most of which have gone to the support of agriculture, have amounted to nearly $46,000,000.

More than 130,000,000 acres have been applied to the work of the common schools of the country, to which the Government has added more than $22,000,000 in special grants from time to time. Many of the states used a portion of the grants to form a permanent school fund, to which they have made material additions so that at the beginning of the century the resulting annual income was more than $10,000,000. At first a large part of the grants was expended for every conceivable educational purpose, including the purchase of school grounds and buildings. Today the proceeds are almost universally applied to the salaries of teachers in every kind of public school work, both elementary and high. While most of it has gone to the support of general education, an increasing amount is being devoted, as they develop, to elementary agriculture, manual training and household arts, and in a few cases to a thoroughgoing training in agriculture and the trades and industries. There is no phase or kind of education—general, social, physical, civic, or vocational—for which some of the moneys given out of the larger bounty of the nation has not been used.

Aside from cash grants, almost 15,000,000 acres have been given for the benefit of our state universities and state agricultural and mechanical colleges.

Grants for Special Kinds of Schools. For aid to special schools such as those for the deaf, dumb, and blind, and reform schools, Congress has given to the states varying quantities of land, totaling more than 2,500,000 acres, and has passed many special acts making appropriations for the benefit of individual schools and colleges, some of them conducted under private agencies.

Grants for Training Teachers. University grants founded many of our state universities, sixty-eight state universities, state colleges, and agricultural and mechanical colleges having been endowed or founded by congressional land grants. These same universities and colleges are today largely supplying the demand for regular high school teachers in the country and are the largest source of supply for teachers, supervisors, and directors of agricultural subjects in our secondary schools. Normal schools have expended the national revenue derived from a million and a half of acres for the preparation of teachers, many of whom have gone out to service in the teaching of elementary agriculture, manual training, or home economics in the common schools of the country.

For many years the work of the agricultural and mechanical colleges, stimulated and supported in part by federal aid, was devoted almost exclusively to education for leadership in agriculture and the mechanical arts. Through experiment station and farm demonstration work, which has been largely a growth of the last decade, these colleges have reached and benefited the farmer at work on his home acres by information and practical illustration. The farm extension work already successfully under way in some of the states is sure to grow rapidly under the stimulus provided by the grant through the Smith-Lever Act, which will in a few years amount to $4,580,000 annually and will thus enable the agricultural and mechanical colleges to greatly extend their field of influence to the mature farmer. What is needed, as will be discussed more fully at another point, is a system of agricultural education in our rural schools, particularly our rural high schools, which will supplement the Smith-Lever Act by training boys and girls for the duties of the farm at the time when they are most teachable and most need to be attracted to the possibilities of a scientific and prosperous agriculture.

The excellent departments of civil, electrical, and mechanical engineering of the agricultural and mechanical colleges have reached and trained technical leaders, whose value to the industry cannot be overestimated. But they have made no pretense of meeting the vocational needs of the mechanic or foreman. Here, again, the service which the agricultural and mechanical colleges and the engineering schools of the country are rendering must be supplemented, as will be demonstrated later, by national grants stimulating our towns and cities to provide, at public expense, industrial and trade education for the great mass of wageworkers.

National grants to federal departments and bureaus which have been used to promote and to aid vocational education in the states are not, of course, included in the statements given. In the past decade, millions of dollars have been expended through the various departments and bureaus of the National Government, for collecting and disseminating this information. While this has been of value to the states, there are rich by-products which have gone to waste, and which would be of inestimable value to the furtherance of vocational education throughout the country if the Government should formulate a plan of cooperation between the bureaus and provide sufficient funds to carry on certain lines of their work with a more specific application to educational purposes.

Vocational Education Grants Are Justified by Results. The opposition to the various bills disbursing federal moneys among the states for educational purposes has been due to fear lest such a policy should make the states dependent upon the Federal Government for the discharge of what is primarily their responsibility of training their own citizens. President Buchanan vetoed the first bill creating the state agricultural and mechanical colleges, because he feared it would "cause the states to lean upon the National Government for the support of their own educational systems." The result of every national grant for education has been quite different. For every dollar of income from federal sources expended by the nation on the common schools of the country in 1910–11, the states themselves spent more than $4, and the states and local governments combined approximately, $26.[13]

The states spent more than four times as much money for higher education as they received in that year from the "Federal Government."[14] In the half century since the establishment of the "land-grant colleges," the large gifts from the United States Treasury for their work have been liberally supplemented by state appropriations, state and local tax levies, and income from state endowment funds. For the five years 1908–12 combined, the total state aid received by the agricultural and mechanical colleges amounted to $58,271,060; the total federal aid to $14,849,969. The federal aid was approximately one-fourth as great as the state aid.[15]

[13] *Report of Commissioner of Education for 1912*, Vol. II, Table 12.

[14] *Ibid.*, Vol. II, p. 360.

[15] *Ibid.*, Vol. II, p. 335.

In the states formed after the close of the Revolutionary War, the national grants for the common schools set forward the cause of public school education "free as the living waters" fully half a century. Federal moneys employed in founding and supporting state universities, providing free training for leadership in civic and professional life, set standards in culture and efficiency in a pioneer period, the results of which cannot be overestimated. The fact is that in most of the states along the eastern coast, where land grants were not available for the stimulation of state universities, such institutions never would have been established. This goes to show that without the aid of the National Government, it is probable that many more of the states would yet be without them as an integral part of a free educational system.

Probably no aid given by the National Government for education has ever proved so fruitful as have these grants for colleges of agriculture and mechanic arts. Instead of causing the states to lean upon the Government for the support of their educational systems, as feared by President Buchanan, the result has been the opposite. New and vigorous colleges have been created. Small and feeble state institutions have been awakened into new life. The agricultural and engineering professions have been developed. The states have been stimulated to make large and rapidly increasing appropriations to these colleges and to their state universities.[16]

National cooperation with the states for vocational education is justified by the precedents in cooperation already established for other important purposes as well as for education. The limits of this report will not permit the treatment of these, which their importance and significance would otherwise require. The Federal Government is acting in cooperation with the states in doing many things which otherwise would remain undone or be but slowly and imperfectly done. The Government carries on many enterprises permitted by the Constitution and necessary to the general welfare which are interstate in interest and character and which could not be conducted satisfactorily by the separate states. The operation of the postal and custom services, the improvement of rivers and harbors, the regulation of navigation and of railroads, the protection and preservation of forests at the headwaters and navigable streams, the reclamation of arid lands, and the protection of migratory birds are examples.

Sometimes appropriations have been made to the states, almost entirely without restrictions, to stimulating them, particularly in pioneer days, toward more rapid development. These appropriations included both grants for the specific benefit of common school and higher education and the more general grants of lands and funds not only for schools but for the laying out and maintaining of roads, the building of bridges and levees, the establishing of proper drainage, the erecting of public buildings, the carrying on of other internal improvements, the encouragement of colonization, the extinction of the state debt, and for any other purpose that the state saw fit.

It might be said in passing that grants of this character have been almost entirely confined to what might be called the period of pioneer development of this country. Not since the middle of the last century have disbursements of money for general purposes been made to the states, nor, in general, have grants for any

---

[16] Monroe, *Cyclopedia of Education*, Vol. IV, p. 380.

purpose been made since that date unaccompanied by requirements insuring joint support by state and nation and reasonable safeguards in the use of the funds. All the moneys now being disbursed to the states are expended in cooperation with them under conditions insuring joint support, as well as proper use of the funds and success of the work benefited.

Human Problem Most Important. This nation is spending more than a billion dollars annually, almost all of which is being used to meet such purely physical problems as the national defense, the promotion of commerce, the operation of the postal and custom services, the preservation of law and order, the erection of public buildings, the improvement of rivers and harbors, and the reclamation of arid lands. Important and necessary as are these services, the proposal to give a modest amount to the states for vocational education of our workers is vastly more so, in proportion as the human problem is greater than the physical. We have done much in the outreach of the federal power for the encouragement of things which, although obvious, are relatively superficial as compared with the need for the practical education of 25,000,000 untrained people, who reach to the very heart of our body politic and weaken or strengthen our social structure.

It would be of little use to have federal aid for good roads or other material benefits making for our physical well-being, if at the same time this country has an uncounted army of untrained workmen and workwomen to carry in life. If we can get our great human force trained and operating along educated lines, all other things will come in a normal manner. To assert year after year the policy of national grants for the purpose of conducting our business and at the same time to neglect the proper preparation of our people is "to set the seen above the unseen."

CHAPTER VI

The Smith-Hughes Act (1917)

Report Submitted to Congress. On June 1, 1914, the Commission on National Aid to Vocational Education submitted a report to Congress which terminated in a chapter entitled "Proposed Legislation." That chapter resulted in a bill embodying the recommendations of the Commission concerning federal aid to the states for vocational education.

Two features of the Report played no small part in the favorable attitude of both Congress and the public toward the work of the Commission. Its findings and recommendations were reported on the date set by Congress (June 1, 1914). Of the $15,000 appropriated for the expenses of the Commission, $5,000 was returned unused.

The submission of the Report ended action during the 64th Congress (1914). No attempt was made to have the Report considered, but plans were laid for a vigorous attempt to pass a bill providing federal aid for vocational education by the 64th Congress (1915). Meanwhile, the full report of the Commission was printed by the Government. The document was given wide circulation, and its recommendations had the support of the public.

Following traditional procedure, the Commission's proposed bill was referred to Senator Hoke Smith of Georgia, chairman of the Senate Committee on Education, and to Congressman Dudley M. Hughes, chairman of the House Committee on Education. Both had been members of the Commission. Both were staunch supporters of free public vocational education, and were skilled in congressional procedure. They became sponsors of the Report and its legislative program by copying verbatim the Bill of the Commission providing federal aid, and introducing it to their respective committees as the Smith-Hughes Bill. Both men used the original draft of their bill to make "corrections, adjustments, concessions, and compromises where necessary" before finally putting the Smith-Hughes Bill on its passage through Congress.

Chamber of Commerce to the Rescue. The Chamber of Com-

Hoke Smith   Dudley M. Hughes

Co-Authors of the Smith-Hughes Act

merce of the United States had always taken a keen interest in national education, and particularly in vocational education. It kept in close contact with the office of the National Society for the Promotion of Vocational Education. Alarmed by the long delay in bringing the Vocational Education Bill to a vote by Congress, the Chamber's national committee on education finally took action.

In February, 1916, a favorable report on the Smith-Hughes Bill was made by the Chamber's committee on education in which it was proposed that the Chamber also hold a nation-wide referendum among affiliate bodies on the Bill.

Begun in April, the report of the results was published in June. The referendum submitted four recommendations to the membership as a means of discovering, by ballot, the attitude of its members toward the Smith-Hughes Bill then pending before Congress.

The President's Concern. No one was more concerned over the delay of national legislation for vocational education than President Wilson. Behind the scenes he viewed with growing consternation the possibility that the United States might become involved, as eventually it did, in the First World War. While the President was careful not to express this fear openly, he saw the great value of a nation-wide preparedness program covering any contingency. Consequently he became as enthusiastic a supporter of vocational education, and of government aid for its support as had Theodore Roosevelt.

In his annual address to Congress on December 7, 1915, President Wilson again stressed the preparedness program and the need for industrial, "vocational," and agricultural education, declaring, "What is important is that the industries and resources of the country should be made available and ready for mobilization. It is the more imperatively necessary, therefore, that we should promptly devise means for doing what we have not yet done; that we should give intelligent federal aid and stimulation to industrial and vocational educational legislation as we have long done in the large field of our agricultural industry."

On January 27, 1916, the President made a second preparedness statement in an address to Congress, saying, "There are two sides to the question of preparation. There is not merely the military side; there is the industrial side. An ideal which I have in mind is this: We ought to have in this great country a system of industrial and vocational education under federal guidance and with federal aid, in which a very large percentage of the youth of the country will be given training in the skillful use and application of the principles of success in maneuver and business."

For more than two years after the Smith-Hughes Bill was presented to Congress, that body apparently gave little outside evidence of interest either in vocational education or in the President's appeals. The *Congressional Record* shows, however, that both houses displayed an unusual interest in national aid to vocational education and in both committee and assembly gave greater attention to it than to almost any other matter. They believed that the program of education for all American youth—which they hoped to put on its way—"will develop as nothing else the human as well as the national resources of the nation."

Congress had paid little attention to either of the President's messages. But neither house could ignore the third appeal made by the President in his annual address to Congress on December 5, 1916, in which he said:

"At the last session of the Congress a bill was passed by the Senate which provides for the promotion of vocational and industrial education; and which is of vital importance to the whole country because it concerns a matter too long neglected, upon which the thorough industrial preparation for the critical years of economic development immediately ahead of us in very large measure depends. May I not urge its early and favorable consideration by the House of Representatives and its early enactment into law. It contains plans which affect all interests and all parts of the country, and I am sure that there is no legislation now pending before the Congress whose passage the country awaits with more thoughtful approval or greater impatience to see a great and admirable thing set in the way of being done."

Ten months after the adoption of the National Vocational Education Act (1917) all of the 48 states had accepted its provisions. Forty-one states did this through a resolution passed by the legislature and signed by the governor. In the remaining seven states, however, the legislature did not meet in 1917, but the Act itself authorized the governor to accept its provisions until the next legislature had met (in 1918) and been in session for 60 days. This gave ample time for the next legislature to confirm the governor's action, insuring in the meantime the federal subsidy for 1917.

Very little has been said regarding the contribution of the various states to the campaign for the legal conservation of American youth. In their legislation establishing state systems of vocational education provision was made by all of the states for full-time schooling up to age sixteen and for the part-time schooling of employed youth beyond that age.

Obviously these laws would be fruitless unless dovetailed into the state compulsory attendance and child labor laws. Notable for this contribution were the laws adopted by Wisconsin and Ohio regulating the education as well as the work of youth under 18 years of age.

Throughout the nation, state legislation for the vocational training of minors had thus far proved far more potent in the control of child labor and schooling than had the attempt to regulate child labor from Washington through an amendment to the Constitution which would have required the favorable vote of at least two-thirds of the states, and for which, as shown by the records, no state had thus far voted.

There was prompt response to President Wilson's appeal for action. In the House of Representatives, the Smith-Hughes (Vocational Education) Bill was given a privileged status. By a shrewd parliamentary procedure the House passed a bill amending the original Smith-Hughes Bill. As the provisions of this Bill differed from those of the provisions of the Senate Bill, they were both sent to joint conference, where a compromise was made to which both Houses agreed. On February 23, 1917—almost three years after the Commission had submitted its Report—President Wilson signed the Vocational Education Act.

Since in the conference the provisions of the House Bill prevailed, the following description of the compromise made by the conference is taken from the statement of Representative Hughes to the House:

1. "The original measure, as it passed the House, included the field of home economics in the appropriations under the trade and industrial funds. The Senate receded from its objections to this provision.

2. "As there are six states (Alabama, Kentucky, Louisiana, Maryland, Mississippi, and Virginia) whose legislatures did not meet in 1917, this fact was brought to the attention of the conferences by senators and representatives from those states. The conferees have endeavored so to shape Section 5 of the Bill that it 'will be possible for these states to accept the provisions of this Act through their governors until their legislators have had time to act.'

3. "The measure, as it passed the Senate, provided that the Federal Board for Vocational Education be composed of the Postmaster General, the Secretary of the Interior, the Secretary of Agriculture, the Secretary of Commerce, and the Secretary of Labor. The Board was authorized to select an advisory board of seven members. A number of experts and specialists were also authorized to assist the Board.

4. "The measure as it passed the House provided for the appointment by the President of a representative of manufacturing interests, a representative of commercial interests other than manufacturing, a representative of labor, and a representative of agriculture to act with the United States Commissioner of Education as a board of five to administer the Act and provide for the employment of such assistants as might be necessary.

"The provision agreed to by the conferees is a blending of the two proposals so that the new system was to be linked with the Government by the designation of the Secretary of Agriculture, the Secretary of Commerce, the Secretary of Labor, and the Commissioner of Labor as ex officio members of the Board and the appointment by the President, with the advice and consent of the Senate, of a representative of manufacturing and commercial interests, a representative of the agricultural interests, and a representative of labor, to act with them as members of the Board.

5. "The House receded from its amendments to the Bill, which had the effect of merely 'authorizing' the appropriations, and the appropriations were definitely made in the Bill as reported from conference."[1]

Following this final report of the agreement between the two Houses, Representative Hughes and, later, Senator S. D. Fess were asked to make a statement—for the *Congressional Record*—stressing the importance of national aid to vocational education. Statement follows:

"This legislation, Mr. Speaker, aims to reach that great mass of our citizenry which is unmoved by our present system and by the offer of the self-help which comes from the proper education and training of head and hand to insure a gradual elevation from the lower to the higher levels of mankind without changing from vocation to profession. We are not so foolish as to claim everything for it. It cannot be a cure for all the ills to which our body politic is heir. We do not hope by legislation to abolish thriftlessness, to eliminate indolence, to inhibit failure or to banish poverty. These we will have with us always. But we do propose to make it easier to succeed and more difficult to fail. We propose here to open the road and point the way. When that is assured something worth while will have been accomplished. Whatever else may be the function of government the materialization of the potentialities of its collective citizenry must ever be one of the chief concerns as well as supreme functions of national sovereignty."

As early as February 16, 1917, the two Houses in joint conference had agreed to the provisions of the Vocational Education (Smith-Hughes) Bill. It did not become a law until approved by

[1] *Congressional Record* (February 16, 1917), p. 3426.

the President on February 23, 1917. That week the National Society held its annual convention in Indianapolis. The customary Thursday night banquet of the convention was held at the Claypool Hotel. Secretary of Commerce William C. Redfield, the president of the Society, and an intimate friend of President Wilson, was unable to attend. He knew that everybody there would be anxiously hoping for good news from Washington. When he explained the situation to the President and suggested that the Bill be signed on Thursday so that the glad news could be sent to the Convention that night, the President promptly declared that "the Act will not go into effect until 1918 and a few days delay in signing will do no harm."

On the twenty-third, the Secretary wired toastmaster James P. Munroe. Mr. Munroe interrupted the speaker. No more speeches were made that night.

When the Convention resumed business the next morning, rejoicing gave way to discussion of the difficult task ahead, and to recognition of a common responsibility for making the vocational movement a success in the face of grave difficulties present and to come.

"Chief among them (the difficulties) were, and still are, the constantly recurring and conflicting interests that need to be harmonized. There is the conflict of ideals between those who seek more practical education—a better adjustment to real life—and those who fear that vocational education will lower the standards of academic education. And there is still the old conflict between a unit versus a dual system of education, and between aristocracy and liberalism in a democratic society."

Mr. Lloyd E. Blauch closed his description of the enactment of the Smith-Hughes Act with the following statement:

"Thus ten years after the introduction of the first Davis Bill, the attempt to obtain federal aid for vocational education below college grade ended. The agitation and discussion had gone on vigorously. At no time did defeat seem on the way. The movement had its beginning in the minds of a comparatively few men. As the years passed, it gathered strength through an increasing number of adherents until, in the later years, a relatively large following had been developed and organized. The strong support eventually produced the results desired for those who demanded federal aid for vocational education."[2]

With only one dissenting vote, the Vocational Education Act had been adopted. With the exception of a change in the federal administrative authority, this Act has remained virtually unchanged for more than three decades. Subsequent acts have increased the national appropriations to the states for vocational education and added new fields and types of training not provided in the original measure.

The real author of the Smith-Hughes Act was the Commission on National Aid to Vocational Education. The Commission's report was submitted to Congress almost three years before the adoption of the Act embodying its recommendations. The Report stated the case for a national program and proposed a bill incorporating the ideas of the Commission regarding establishment of the program.

In turn, the Vocational Education Act achieved three ends for the Commission: (1) It encouraged the states to undertake for their citizens a new and vital kind of education in cooperation with the Federal Government; (2) it provided federal funds to aid the states and their local communities in meeting the cost of the new educational service; and (3) it safeguarded the expenditure of federal money for training by establishing the same minimum standards for all the states, and by requiring that the money be used for the purposes designated.

The outcome of the cooperative teamplay between the Federal Board and the states and their schools is best illustrated by a statement of what had been accomplished by them for vocational education. The statement was made in a news letter of the National Society for Vocational Education, issued in June, 1922:

1. Before January 1, 1918, every state in the Union had accepted the provisions of the National Vocational Education Act.

2. During the same period every state in the Union submitted plans for accepting the provisions of the Federal Act and the rulings of the Federal Board for Vocational Education.

3. Every state in the Union designated or created a definite state board for the administration of vocational education.

[2] Charles A. Bennett, *Manual and Industrial Education* (Peoria, Ill., Chas. A. Bennett Press, Inc., 1937), Vol. II, p. 550. Out of print.

4. In 1916 only two states in the Union—Wisconsin and Pennsylvania—had compulsory part-time or continuation school laws. As a result of the Smith-Hughes Act, all states now have compulsory part-time education laws.

5. The total of all expenditures for vocational education in schools subsidized from federal funds increased from $2,683,639.52 in 1918 to the sum of $10,649,-852.11 in 1920–21. The far-reaching influence of the Vocational Education Act is indicated further by the very large increase in appropriations for vocational education work by local communities, viz., from the sum of $1,201,542.38 in 1918 to $5,182,818.22 in 1921.[3]

6. The enrollment in federally aided vocational schools increased from 164,-186 in 1917 to 323,028 in 1921.

7. The number enrolled in federally subsidized teacher-training courses increased from 6,589 in 1918 to 13,358 in 1921.

Relation of Vocational Act to Subsequent Acts. The Vocational Education Act was the culmination of an evolution in national appropriations for vocational education. Beginning with the Morrill Act of 1862, the Federal Government has, by successive acts—the Hatch Act, the second Morrill Act of 1890, the Adams Act, the Nelson Amendment, the Smith-Lever Act, and the Vocational Education (Smith-Hughes) Act—gradually found a sound philosophy and policy in the use of national money for vocational purposes. The Morrill Act imposed few conditions in the use of money by the states. The Smith-Lever Act imposed many conditions. It is safe to say that the Vocational Education Act is the most specific and exacting of all these enactments in its requirements upon the states in the use of federal money.

---

[3] The *Congressional Record* shows that in all the increase of the federal subsidy not one cent of it has been lost by theft or misuse—an unanswerable indictment of "pork barrel" and omnibus legislation.

CHAPTER VII

The Administration of the Smith-Hughes Act — State Plans

A PARTNERSHIP IN EDUCATION

In other chapters we have referred to the "partnership" between the states[1] and the federal government formed through the provisions of the Smith-Hughes Act. We have referred at various times to the contractural relations existing between these two agencies, in which each state agreed to do or not to do some particular thing or things for a given consideration. The consideration was an allotment of federal funds appropriated by Congress.

The idea of "partnership" or agreement apparently had its genesis between 1910 and 1912. The early bills introduced in the House of Representatives by Congressman Davis of Minnesota, and in the Senate by Senators Dolliver of Iowa and Page of Vermont, did not refer to any kind of a *plan* as a condition of participation in the benefits of federal funds appropriated for vocational education.

The first reference to a plan seems to have been in the revision of S-3, a bill introduced by Senator Page on April 6, 1911. The bill was referred to the Committee on Agriculture and Forestry. On August 14, 1911, the Committee submitted its report with a number of amendments, one of which was inserted in the original Section 5 (new Section 4). It provided that the funds appropriated for college-extension departments or divisions should be used only under a plan approved by state directors of state experimental stations.[2]

Eight months later Congressman William B. Wilson, who as Secretary of Labor, 1917–21, was ex officio a member of the Federal Board, improved on the idea when he introduced H.R. 23581 on April 10, 1912. He inserted a provision in Section 18 making a state plan a condition of approval. Under this provision, which read, "the board for vocational education for each state and the District of Columbia shall adopt, with the approval of the Secre-

---

[1] The term "state" is intended to include the territories of Alaska and Hawaii, the Island of Puerto Rico, and the District of Columbia, as well as the 48 states.

[2] Senate Report No. 405, 62d Congress, 2d Session, p. 73.

tary of the Interior, and place in operation a general administrative scheme or plan" for the administration of the Act. This new language was discussed by Dr. C. A. Prosser at the hearings on the bill held on April 24, 1912, in much the same language used by him two years later at the meeting of the Commission on National Aid to Vocational Education held on April 23, 1914. Then, in response to a suggestion made by Miss Leonora O'Reilly, representing the Women's Trade Union League, Dr. Prosser, addressing Miss O'Reilly, asked:

"What would you think of this method of carrying out the suggestion you made? Suppose that a federal statute were drawn giving *grants* to the states, under certain broad conditions, this *money* to be disbursed by the states through *state boards of control*, selected by the states—in most cases the State Board of Education—then to have the federal statute set up a *working relation* between the *National Board* or *national authority* and the state boards of control for the states. The state board would come to the National Board and say· 'The conditions in our state are such that we recommend this *Plan*, which we want to try out.'[3]

"When the representatives of the state and the nation came to a meeting of minds on any plan adopted to meet state conditions, then the state board of control, entirely free from the National Government, would put it into operation. The state would receive the annual amount due it and give it out to approved schools in the state, coming back for further discussion only when it made changes in its plan. In this way the state would receive grants from the national government as long as it carried out the *terms of the partnership* set up between the nation and the state. Would not a plan of that kind provide for the things which this Commission has in mind?"

Miss O'Reilly agreed that it would.

Agencies of Cooperation. When the Federal Board for Vocational Education issued its *Statement of Policies*[4] in 1917 it said, "The machinery established by the Act is devised to secure effective cooperation in promoting vocational education. The law provides for the appointment by the President of a representative Federal Board for Vocational Education. It also provides for administrative agencies representing the states. The Act requires that state boards of

---

[3] Italics used for emphasis upon essential characteristics of the proposal.
[4] *Statement of Policies* (1917 ed.), Bulletin No. 1, p. 7.

not less than three members shall be created by state legislation. Each state board is to work in cooperation with the Federal Board in carrying out the provisions of the Act.

"The scheme of education proposed contemplates that each state shall submit to the Federal Board a plan outlining the method by which it proposes to conduct its vocational education activities. These plans the Federal Board must carefully examine. If it finds them to be in conformity with the spirit and purpose of the Act, it is authorized to direct that the moneys apportioned to the various states be paid. In other words, partly by the Act itself, partly by the Federal Board, and partly by the state board in cooperation with the Federal Board, standards of vocational education are established meeting the approbation of both the state and federal governments. Each in its own field supreme, the state board and the Federal Board, in order to function at all, must come together on the ground thus briefly described."

Growth of an Idea. More than a third of a century has elapsed since Dr. Prosser discussed his idea of a state plan as the medium which would cement the partnership between the national and state governments in a cooperative program of vocational education. His idea was later incorporated by the Commission in its report to Congress. Congress wrote it into the Smith-Hughes Act, thereby making it a part of the *basic law*. The Federal Board incorporated the basic law with its interpretations in the *Statement of Policies* issued to the states. The state boards wrote their plans in conformity with the basic law and the policies of the federal office. The local school authorities organized their vocational school programs under the provisions of the state plan.

The state plan, when thus conceived, written, and approved, becomes, for the time being, the contract or agreement between the federal and state authorities. It assures the state complete freedom from federal interference in administration of the program. It assures the federal office that the money which Congress appropriated for specific purposes will be properly expended so long as the state does not violate the provisions of its plan. Finally, it provides the local schools with a set of "specifications" to use in building their programs of vocational education if they desire to be reimbursed by the state for salaries paid their teachers. If the local school authorities are not interested in reimbursement, they are free to follow or not to follow the provisions of the state plan.

PREPARATION OF STATE PLANS

The authors of this book were all members of the original executive staff of the Federal Board for Vocational Education when it was organized in 1917. One of them had continuous responsibility for assisting the states in the preparation of their plans, and in reviewing them for the fiscal period, 1917–47. The preparation of state plans is, therefore, a matter of record, memory, and first-hand experience. Official records on file in the U.S. Office of Education contain the plans as submitted, the dates of their submission, and approval with files of correspondence relating thereto. What they do not show are some of the early experiences gained by members of the federal and state staffs in the development of a state plan over a period of thirty years. This experience is recorded only in individual memories.

The fact that only six or seven states had state laws in operation providing some form of state aid to vocational education in advance of the Smith-Hughes Act did not add much to their experience in writing state plans. Therefore, all states "started from scratch." The difference was that a few states had the benefit of experience in the administration of vocational schools and classes and knew more about the aims, objectives, types of schools and philosophy of vocational education.

First State Plans Hastily Prepared. The Federal Board held its first meeting on July 21, 1917. It met in conference with chief state school officers in August to discuss what the states must do to qualify for participation in the moneys already appropriated by Congress. During the last week in September, it was able to hold a series of interoffice conferences with its executive staff, including the regional agents.

At these interoffice conferences the Board, director, and assistant directors gave instructions to the newly appointed regional agents and sent them out into their respective regions to assist the states in completing their acceptances of the federal Act, and in drafting a state plan based upon the conditions and needs of the state. The Federal Board had set the goal—all states to be qualified for certification of their allotments by January 1, 1918. That meant completing forty-eight state plans in three months. A few states had made some progress, and some had sent preliminary plans for review, but not one plan had been processed by the executive staff and submitted to the Board for approval.

Topical Outline of State Plans. A brief topical outline was prepared for the information of the state boards to assist them in preparing their plans with reasonable uniformity. This topical outline later was issued to the states with Circular Letter No. 100. For many years the outline and letter were known as *C.L. 100.*

In 1917 the regional agents for agricultural and trade and industrial education traveled in pairs within their respective regions. Appointments were made by telegram and each state was given as much time as needed to discuss the program, make a brief survey of its needs and prepare its plan in fairly complete form for the consideration of the state board. These activities would take from four to six days in each state after which the federal agent moved on to the next state. It was a "catch as catch can" procedure in making appointments and being able to keep them with state officials. As they traveled from state to state they gained experience. They became more familiar with the aims, purposes and provisions of the basic Act, and were better able to assist the states in getting started.

There was wide variation in state plans when first submitted to the Federal Board. One state visited by an agent announced, "Oh, we have our plan all written. We have had it printed and are ready to send it in for approval." On examination it was found that the plan as printed occupied two pages of an 8½ x 11 sheet of paper. It was only a brief outline of the requirements enumerated in the Smith-Hughes Act. Other state plans were voluminous. They were replete with printed catalogues and courses of study of teacher-training institutions.

All of these first plans, voluntarily prepared in advance of any action on the part of the staff of the Federal Board, showed the need for a topical outline which would provide a degree of uniformity among the states in its form and arrangement of subjects, and which would govern the length of state plans.

The first topical outline, hastily prepared, has been revised from time to time until it now represents a model for plans of like character and purpose. The practice of calling this outline "C.L. 100" became quite general. In later years an effort was made to change the short title to the longer and more exact one of *Topical Outline for State Plans for Vocational Education*. The latest revision was issued on November 30, 1946, and transmitted to the states with C.L. 2609.

Completion of State Plans. With 48 states and three months to go, the task of getting all plans in and approved by January 1, 1918, seemed almost superhuman. Yet, within the time limit every one of the 48 states had accepted the Act, prepared and secured approval of its plan, and complied with all necessary requirements for establishing a state system of vocational education in cooperation with the national government.

Approval of State Plans for 1917 and 1918. At its meeting on October 18, 1917, the Federal Board gave formal approval to the first group of state plans recommended by the executive staff and the standing committee. The minutes read:

VOTED: That the chairman be authorized to certify the following seven states as entitled to receive the first quarterly allotment from the appropriations for salaries of teachers of agricultural subjects, the appropriation for the salaries of teachers of trade, home economics, and industrial subjects, and the appropriation for the training of teachers, supervisors, or directors of agricultural subjects, or of teachers of trade, industrial, or home economics subjects as provided by an Act of Congress approved February 23, 1917: Arizona, Arkansas, California, Maine, New York, Pennsylvania, and Utah.

VOTED: That the chairman be authorized to certify the State of Texas as entitled to receive the first quarterly allotment from the appropriation for the salaries of teachers, supervisors, or directors of agricultural subjects, as provided by an Act of Congress approved February 23, 1917.

For the benefit of readers who desire information of similar character for all of the states, Table I is presented to show the manner in which the states accepted the National Vocational Education Act, the date when the State Acceptance Act became effective, and the date of approval by the Federal Board of the first state plan of each of the states.

State Plans Are Live Instruments. The most fundamental characteristic of vocational education is that it is built around the training needs of the individual, of the job, and of society. As these needs grow and change with time, so, also, must the training program grow and change. This means that vocational programs must be kept *flexible*, alive and adapted to changing needs and economic conditions. The state plan, the instrument in which the state board sets forth the kinds of schools it proposes to promote with the aid of federal funds, must also live, grow, and develop in step with these changing needs and economic conditions.

Five-Year Period for Submission of Plans. During the five-year period, 1917–22, the states revised and resubmitted their plans annually. Each year they were rewritten, approved by the state board, and then transmitted to the Federal Board for approval.

In 1922 the Federal Board suggested a change in this procedure and, accordingly, asked the states to prepare and submit their plans for a five-year period with the understanding that any state could propose an amendment to its plan at any time, and that the amendment would be received and accorded the same consideration for approval it would have been given had it been a part of the original plan.

Most states complied with this suggestion. During the years many amendments have been submitted. These amendments have served to keep the state plan alive and flexible to meet any emergency.

AMENDMENTS TO STATE PLANS

The Constitution of the United States, carefully written during the summer of 1787 by the delegates from the 12 states attending the convention in Philadelphia, and signed by 39 of the 55 members in attendance, originally consisted of a preamble and seven articles. Even before it had been ratified by the necessary nine states and declared in effect by the Government on the first Wednesday in March, 1789, a number of "safeguarding" amendments were proposed for submission to the people. Twelve such amendments were submitted to the first Congress meeting in the city of New York on September 25, 1789, and ten of these original amendments were adopted.

Without the power to amend the Constitution it is a question how long our democracy would have endured. The original ten amendments were more or less routine and perfunctory. They represented issues already before the people, most of which, no doubt, were debated by the delegates to the Constitutional Convention. During the period of 161 years since the ten original amendments[5] were ratified by the states, eleven more have been added. We question whether many of them would have been approved by the voters of 1791. For example, the XVI Amendment authorized income taxation, and the XIX Amendment gave nation-wide suffrage to women. These issues came before the people over a period of many years. During this time public opinion had crystallized in favor of a change in fundamental law. In a similar manner, state plans need to be amended from time to time, especially when submitted for five-year periods.

---

[5] The Bill of Rights.

STATE OR TERRITORY	ACT ACCEPTED BY		FIRST STATE PLAN APPROVED
	Proclamation of the Governor [a]	Act of State Legislature	
Alabama	Sept. 5, 1917	Feb. 15, 1919	Dec. 14, 1917
Arizona		March 12, 1917	Oct. 18, 1917
Arkansas		March 6, 1917	Oct. 18, 1917
California		May 31, 1917	Oct. 18, 1917
Colorado		April 10, 1917	Dec. 14, 1917
Connecticut		May 17, 1917	Dec. 28, 1917
Delaware		April 2, 1917	Nov. 9, 1917
Florida		June 5, 1917	Dec. 14, 1917
Georgia		[b]	Nov. 9, 1917
Idaho	Oct. 31, 1917	March 14, 1919	Dec. 28, 1917
Illinois	Nov. 14, 1917	March 6, 1919	Dec. 28, 1917
Indiana		March 7, 1917	Dec. 14, 1917
Iowa		April 23, 1917	Dec. 14, 1917
Kansas		March 12, 1917	Dec. 14, 1917
Kentucky	Aug. 31, 1917	March 6, 1918	Nov. 9, 1917
Louisiana	Nov. 20, 1917	June 27, 1918	Nov. 9, 1917
Maine		[c]	Oct. 18, 1917
Maryland	[d] Oct. 5, 1917	April 10, 1918	Dec. 28, 1917
Massachusetts		May 2, 1917	Nov. 9, 1917
Michigan		May 5, 1917	Dec. 14, 1917
Minnesota		April 21, 1917	Dec. 14, 1917
Mississippi	Sept. 14, 1917	Oct. 11, 1917	Dec. 14, 1917
Missouri		March 15, 1917	Dec. 28, 1917
Montana		March 5, 1917	Dec. 14, 1917
Nebraska		[e] March 24, 1919	Dec. 14, 1917
Nevada		March 24, 1917	Nov. 9, 1917
New Hampshire		April 19, 1917	Dec. 28, 1917
New Jersey		March 24, 1917	Nov. 9, 1917
New Mexico		May 5, 1917	Nov. 9, 1917
New York		May 21, 1917	Oct. 18, 1917
North Carolina		[f] March 5, 1919	Dec. 14, 1917
North Dakota	Dec. 8, 1917	March 4, 1919	Dec. 28, 1917
Ohio		March 30, 1917	Dec. 14, 1917
Oklahoma		March 24, 1917	Nov. 9, 1917
Oregon	May 10, 1917	March 4, 1917	Dec. 14, 1917
Pennsylvania		July 11, 1917	Oct. 18, 1917
Rhode Island	[g] Dec. 31, 1917	April 17, 1918	[h] Dec. 28, 1917
South Carolina		Feb. 27, 1917	Nov. 9, 1917

[a] Section 5 of the Smith-Hughes Act provided for acceptance by proclamation of the governor in states where the state legislature did not meet in 1917. Effective until 60 days after legislature met in regular session.
[b] Georgia: Date of acceptance act not available. A letter from M. L. Brittain to P. P. Claxton, dated August 17, 1917, states; "Herewith send copy of vocational bill which passed the Ga. Legislature—1917 School Legislation."
[c] Maine: Date of acceptance act not available. Approved by the 78th State Legislature, Chapter 186, P.L. 1917.
[d] Maryland: Copy of proclamation not available. Date given is that of a letter from Governor Harrington to P. P. Claxton stating, "I hereby formally accept the act."
[e] Nebraska: Accepted by State Statute in 1917. Date not available.
[f] North Carolina: The purposes of the Smith-Hughes Act were approved by State Statute March 1, 1917.
[g] Rhode Island: Accepted by the Governor insofar as it related to trade and industry.
[h] —— The first State Plan was approved for trade and industry only.

TABLE I–*Continued*

| STATE OR TERRITORY | ACT ACCEPTED BY | | FIRST STATE PLAN APPROVED |
	Proclamation of the Governor	Act of State Legislature	
South Dakota.........	....	March 10, 1917	Dec. 14, 1917
Tennessee.............	....	March 31, 1917	Nov. 9, 1917
Texas................	....	i March 24, 1919	j Oct. 18, 1917
Utah................	....	March 17, 1917	Oct. 18, 1917
Vermont.............	....	March 23, 1917	Dec. 28, 1917
Virginia.............	March 28, 1917	April 9, 1918	Nov. 9, 1917
Washington..........	....	k	Dec. 14, 1917
West Virginia.........	....	May 26, 1917	Nov. 9, 1917
Wisconsin............	....	l	Nov. 9, 1917
Wyoming............	....	Feb. 20, 1917	Dec. 14, 1917
Alaska...............	....	March 14, 1935	May 17, 1935
District of Columbia....	....	m	Dec. 17, 1937
Hawaii..............	April 7, 1924	April 29, 1925	Dec. 4, 1924
Puerto Rico.........	....	April 23, 1931	July 24, 1931

i Texas: Revised acceptance Act. Copy of original acceptance act enclosed with letter of June 6, 1917, from W. F. Doughty to P. P. Claxton was undated.
j ——— Approved for agriculture only. Plan for all purposes approved Dec. 14, 1917.
k Washington: Accepted by an item in the State appropriation Act, p. 834, Session of Laws of 1917. The appropriation became available April 1, 1917, according to a letter from Governor Lister to P. P. Claxton dated June 6, 1917.
l Wisconsin: Date of acceptance not available. Accepted by State legislature in 1917, Chapter 494, laws of 1917, Subsection 4, Section 41.13, Wisconsin Statutes 1917.
m District of Columbia: Acceptance inherent in Act of Congress approved June 8, 1936, providing federal appropriation for vocational education. Solicitor's opinion, Dec. 10, 1937.
Prepared at the request of J. C. Wright by Iva Grace Prisk, Educational Statistician, Vocational Division, U.S. Office of Education.

During the thirty years from 1917 to 1947, the states amended their plans many times. In some instances these amendments were proposed by the federal office, but usually the need was anticipated by the state. In times of national stress, as in the period of the depression and during World War II, a wave of amendments swept the federal office. The majority of these amendments were proposed and approved either for a specified period of time or for the "duration."

Amendments Suggested by Federal Office. As an illustration of amendments suggested by the federal office we cite C.L. 2108, issued on November 1, 1938, to chief state school officers, and state directors of vocational education on the subject of "Amendments to State Plans to Provide for the Maintenance of a State Occupational Information and Guidance Service." In this pronouncement the federal office advised the states that:

Under date of October 28, 1938, the Commissioner of Education authorized the use of federal teacher-training funds, available under the Smith-Hughes and the George-Deen acts, for partial maintenance of State Occupational Information and Guidance services.

In order that these funds may be so used by a state, it will be necessary for the State Board for Vocational Education to submit a plan (or amendment to present approved plan) describing the proposed state program of Occupational Information and Guidance, the duties and qualifications of supervisors, and the amount of federal funds to be used for supervision. If this plan (or amendment) is found to be in conformity with the acts and with the *Statement of Policies* contained in *Bulletin No. 1* (as amended on October 28, 1938), the same will be approved.

Similar suggestions have been made whenever new policies affecting the use of federal funds have been issued. At the July 11, 1918, meeting of the Federal Board the use of teacher-training funds for the maintenance of a program of state supervision was authorized on condition:

"That a plan of supervision be set up by the state board and approved by the Federal Board."

This plan was to include the qualifications of supervisors and provided that not more than twenty-five per cent of the maximum which may be used for teacher training in any one of the three lines —trades and industries, home economics, and agriculture—could be used for the maintenance of supervision in that field. To put this program in operation in any state, it was necessary to amend the state plan. The states quickly responded to this suggestion.

Other suggested amendments related to the training of employees in industrial plants, the use of representative advisory committees, and training for public service.

CHIEF PURPOSES OF STATE PLANS

State plans serve various purposes, some of which are:

1. They represent the contract or agreement between the federal and state authorities.

2. They represent the policy of state boards and as such become official guides for their administrative and supervisory staffs.

3. They furnish information to local school officials necessary to the organization and administration of vocational schools and classes, if reimbursement from federal funds or state funds is to be expected.[6]

4. They insure a continuity in the state program throughout changing administrations.

---

[6] The Pennsylvania Plan for 1947–52 provides for a State-Local Plan of Cooperation which marks a definite trend in this direction.

5. They furnish vital information to teacher-training institutions.

6. They provide a legal basis on which both state and federal field representatives may make administrative decisions.

7. If conscientiously prepared, they cause all members of the professional staffs of state boards to evaluate and justify, at five-year intervals (or more frequently) their particular part of the state's program.

STATEMENT OF POLICY RESPECTING STATE PLANS

In 1917 the Federal Board for Vocational Education included in its *Statement of Policies* a single paragraph consisting of two sentences respecting the subject of state plans.[7] The paragraph referred to reads:

> It is highly desirable that the state propose plans using the federal money for one fiscal year only. In this way they will be able from year to year to improve their plans and standards so as to conform to the development of work and conditions in the states and communities.

In the *Statement of Policies* revised and reissued in May, 1922, the Board's policy had been modified to read:

> During the first few years after the passage of the Act it was highly desirable that the state propose plans using the federal moneys for one fiscal year only. In this way they were able, from year to year, to improve their plans and standards so as to conform to the development of the program and to changing conditions in the states and communities. The work has progressed, however, to such an extent that, beginning July 1, 1922, a state may submit a plan with a request for approval by the Federal Board for a five-year period. . . .

The 1917 and subsequent editions of the *Statement of Policies* contain a statement giving the fundamental philosophy of the federal office with respect to the state plan. In the revision of February, 1937, this statement reads:

COOPERATIVE AGREEMENT OR PLAN BETWEEN THE FEDERAL GOVERNMENT AND A STATE

> The cooperative agreement between the Federal Government and the state is a cooperative agreement with that state and not with all states. It is proposed by a state board for vocational education for a state and is approved by the Office of Education for that state only. It would be impossible to set up a single uniform plan for the country as a whole, which would take adequate account of the differ-

---

[7] *Statement of Policies*, Bulletin No. 1, Item XIV, p. 18.

ing social, economic, and industrial conditions in the several states. In its administrative discretion the Office of Education must decide what arrangement it is willing to enter into with each state as a unit. It should be emphasized that the plan for cooperation is in every case offered by the state board and passed upon by the Office of Education. Authority to disapprove state plans involving reimbursements out of federal money rests with the Office of Education, but this authority does not imply authority to dictate or to initiate state plans in any particular. It implies only authority to determine conditions of reimbursement under the federal acts. Disapproval does not mean that a state may not adopt a plan, but only that it may not use federal funds for reimbursement under the plan disapproved.

The Office of Education will look with favor on those state plans which comply with the spirit as well as the letter of the law. The Smith-Hughes Act provides "for the *promotion* of vocational education"; and the George-Deen Act provides "for the *further development* of vocational education in the several States and Territories." While the Office of Education is interested in assisting states and territories in maintaining the gains that have already been made, it is particularly desirous of cooperating in any program that contemplates the development of vocational education in areas and among groups hitherto not reached. Because of the great need for training among such groups and because they represent such a large proportion of the population in the states, the Office of Education is interested in and desirous of cooperating with the states in working out plans looking toward more adequate programs of vocational education for these groups.

This same general philosophy was included in the latest revision of the official policies on the administration of the national vocational education acts, issued in November, 1947.

LEGAL BASIS FOR STATE PARTICIPATION

The legal basis for a state's participation in the benefits of the national vocational education acts is given in Sections 5 and 8 of the Smith-Hughes Act. Section 8 provides for the submission of a state plan, in the following language:

Section 8. That in order to secure the benefits of the appropriation for any purpose specified in this Act, the state board shall prepare plans, showing the kinds of vocational education for which it is proposed that the appropriation shall be used; the kinds of schools and equipment; courses of study; methods of instruction; qualifications of teachers; and, in the case of agricultural subjects, the qualifications of supervisors or directors; plans for the training of teachers; and, in the case of agricultural subjects, plans for the supervision of agricultural education, as provided for in Section 10. Such plans shall be submitted by the state board to the Federal Board for Vocational Education, and if the Federal Board finds the same to be in conformity with the provisions and purposes of this Act, the same shall be approved.

When the original plans were received in the federal office, the legal basis for state participation was carefully weighed in terms of the three statutory provisions enumerated in Section 5 of the Federal Act and a favorable opinion obtained from the legal counsel of the Federal Board before approving the plan.

In later years it was assumed that the state Act of Acceptance continued to establish the legal basis for cooperation. However, in recent years it was found that in at least one state the passage of a general school law had, according to a written opinion of the attorney general for the state, repealed essential provisions of the Act of Acceptance. Under this opinion there had been no legal basis for state participation in the benefits of the federal acts for more than twenty years. It was necessary for the state to enact new legislation to remove the conflict.

In the case just cited, the federal office had never been notified of the conflicting legislation. To avoid similar conflict in other states the Board provided, in the topical outline, for state plans of the period 1947–52 that individual states should keep the federal office informed on all legislation, court decisions, executive orders, and state attorney general's opinions affecting the right of states to participate in the program.

It also asks the state to accept the responsibility of keeping the federal office informed of current developments that would in any way affect the legality of the state plan.

SOME ABUSES OF STATE PLANS

Throughout the thirty-year period of operation of the cooperative program of vocational education, the state plan has been the bond consolidating the different parts of the program. To be a strong bond it must be kept alive; it must constantly reflect current needs of the state for vocational education, and it must be open to amendment as required in order to protect it from abuses to which it is likely to be subjected. Some of the abuses which have affected its value as a sound foundation for a state vocational program are:

1. Using the plan as a detailed course of study to be imposed on local schools.

2. Using the plan to provide "job tenure" by writing qualifications of personnel around the individual characteristics of one person so that only he can qualify.

3. Failure to publicize the plan and make it available to schools and teachers.

4. Failure to utilize the experience and knowledge of the supervisory staff in making revisions.

5. Failure to tie the plan in with the state Acceptance Act and amendments thereto and thus keep up to date the legal basis for the state's participation in the benefits of the Smith-Hughes Act and all acts supplementary to it.

6. Newly elected or appointed executive officers do not take the time to become informed about the provisions and importance of the plan as a manual and guide for the vocational program. Consequently, in planning a program based upon the needs of the state, they are likely to think of it as a scheme imposed upon the state rather than a fundamental instrument growing out of long experience.

7. Failure to edit amendments into original plans, after approval, and thus keep the plan current and up to date. The federal office has frequently been asked to supply copies of approved amendments when states are revising their plans at the end of a five-year period.

8. Failure to consult with experienced local directors responsible for operating programs.

9. A tendency to look upon the plan as a federal rather than a state plan.

10. Inclusion of too many qualifying and "or the equivalent" phrases in connection with fundamental standards.

CHAPTER VIII

Legislation Supplementary to the Smith-Hughes Act (1917–47)

The events leading up to the promotion and passage of the Smith-Hughes Act of 1917 have been recorded in previous chapters. This Act was the basic federal law into which the framers wrote their philosophy of vocational education of less than college grade. They enumerated the standards which experience demonstrated as the minimum for the states to meet if they were to participate in federal aid for vocational education.

It is a remarkable fact that the basic Act has had but two minor legislative amendments in thirty years. During this time the Federal Government and the states have worked together cooperatively in building a program of vocational education in which nearly three million youth and adults are enrolled annually. In addition, it has been amended three times by executive order under authority granted the President by the Congress.

Legislative Developments, 1900–17. Preceding 1900 the idea had been rapidly crystallizing that federal aid would be necessary to provide that equality of educational opportunity expressed by President Theodore Roosevelt in a letter to Senator Page, of Vermont. Written in 1911, he gave his views on the merits of S-3—"A bill to cooperate with the states in encouraging instruction in agriculture, the trades and industries, and home economics in secondary schools, in maintaining instruction in these vocational subjects in state normal schools; in maintaining extension departments in state colleges of agriculture and mechanic arts; and to appropriate money and regulate its expenditure."[1] In his letter President Roosevelt said:

The passage of this bill would merely be putting into effect that cardinal American doctrine of furnishing a reasonable equality of opportunity and chance

---

[1] *Senate Report 405* (Committee on Agriculture and Forestry, 62d Congress, 2d Session, February 26, 1912).

of development to all our children, wherever they live and whatever may be their station in life. Such a federal cooperation in technical education will help in many ways. It will mean much for country life, for the life of the family farm, for the life of the city workers who seek landed homes in the country near the city in which they work. It will mean much along the lines of the great policy of conservation of the natural resources of our land. Finally, it will mean much to the nation of the future, because it will represent the effort to give exact justice and an equal opportunity for development to each of the boys and girls who in the future are to make up the nation.

Industrial training, training which will fit a girl to do work in the home, which will fit a boy to work in the shop if in the city, to work on a farm if in the country, is the most important of all training aside from that which develops character, and it is a grave reproach to us as a nation that we have permitted our training to lead children away from the farm and shop instead of toward them.[2]

The school system should be aimed primarily to fit the scholar for actual life rather than for the university.

INDEX OF LEGISLATIVE REFERENCES TO VOCATIONAL EDUCATION, 1900–47

The basic facts of the history of federal legislation on any subject are recorded in the *Congressional Record*. They are also found in the various files of bills, reports, resolutions and documents—bound and preserved by the Library of Congress. Historical records of the Legislative Reference Bureau furnished the data from which the accompanying Index of Legislative References on Vocational Education (Tables I and II) was compiled. Facts interesting to students of vocational education may be noted from Table I of the Index.

1. During this 17-year period, no less than 39 bills were introduced in the two Houses of Congress—13 in the Senate and 26 in the House of Representatives. The Senate bills were introduced by seven different senators and the House bills by eleven different congressmen. These senators and congressmen came from fifteen different states of the Union—from the North and South and from the Middle West.

2. At no time during this period was there any organized or mass objection to the general purpose of the proposed legislation. The delay in passing a bill was due largely to the attempt to perfect the language, to a desire to isolate the specific functions which should be included, and to the need of agreeing upon provisions for its administration.

3. In 1901 the idea was to give federal aid to industrial insti-

---

[2] Previous to 1909 the terms *industrial education* and *industrial training* were used synonymously with the terms *vocational education* and *vocational training*, as used today.

tutes having state charters. However, in this same year Senator Knute Nelson, of Minnesota, used the phrase "to *encourage* industrial education in the several states." The phrase "to encourage" marked an advanced step in the evolution of federal aid to vocational education. It opened up a new field of state relations in which the Federal Government would help the states to help themselves and aid in the promotion of new forms of education opportunities. It marked the initial idea of a cooperative program between the Federal Government and the states. It was not until 1909, however, that Congressman Davis, of Minnesota, introduced H. R. 26737, "A bill to cooperate with the states in encouraging instruction in farming and homemaking in agricultural secondary schools with branch experiment stations; instruction in nonagricultural industries and homemaking in city secondary schools; and in providing teachers for these *vocational subjects* in normal schools; and to appropriate money and regulate its expenditure." This bill contained the first reference to "vocational education."

4. During this period the National Society for the Promotion of Industrial Education was organized. On May 7, 1908, Senator Lodge of Massachusetts, introduced a bill (S-7005) to incorporate the National Society. While this bill did not pass it did afford an opportunity for Congress to become acquainted with the views of labor, of employers and of many leading educators regarding the need for federal aid in the promotion of vocational education. Among these leaders were men like William C. Redfield, president of the National Society for five successive years, a former member of Congress, and Secretary of Commerce in the cabinet of President Wilson; Dr. David Snedden, Commissioner of Education in Massachusetts; Dr. Charles R. Richards, of Columbia University; Dr. Charles H. Winslow, of the American Federation of Labor; and many other leaders in business, labor, education, and public service. Many of these leaders were brought before congressional committees to testify and express their views on legislative proposals or were given an opportunity to present their views in writing. A large number of such testimonials were published in the *Congressional Record* and in the reports of public hearings.

5. Perhaps the most important fact of interest to the student delving into the history of vocational education is that of the gradual emergence of legislative proposals which eventually culminated in the Smith-Hughes Act. During the middle years of

TABLE I. INDEX OF LEGISLATIVE REFERENCES—VOCATIONAL EDUCATION (1900–1917)

(Compiled by J. C. Wright, June, 1947)

CONGRESS	SESSION	BILLS INTRODUCED			PAGE REFERENCES TO CONGRESSIONAL RECORD	TITLE OF BILL AND NOTES ON ACTIONS TAKEN BY CONGRESS (A) Referred to Committee on Education and Labor (B) Referred to Committee on Education (X) (C) Referred to Committee on Agriculture and Forestry (X) No further action on Bill
		Bill No.	Date	By Whom		
(1)	(2)	(3)	(4)	(5)	(6)	(7)
56th	2d	S5336	Jan. 3, 1901	Hansbrough, of N.D.	499	A bill to create a Department of Education—to Committee on Education (AX) (The only bill included in this index that did not relate to vocational education.)
57th	1st	S1246	Dec. 9, 1901	Money, of Miss.	214	A bill for the benefit of industrial institutes and schools with State Charters for the education of women (AX)
"	"	S2030	Dec. 18, 1901	Knute Nelson, of Minn.	387	A bill to encourage industrial education in the several States (AX)
"	"	S2031	" 19 "	" " "	387	A bill to encourage industrial education in the Territories and Islands (AX)
"	"	HR7480	" "	Rixey, of Va.	450, 3307	(Same as S2030) (B), reported adversely—H.R. Report 1226
"	"	HR7481	" "	" "	450, 3307	(Same as S2031) " "
"	2d	—				
58th	2d	HR14970	Apr. 11, 1904	Rixey, of Va.	4668	A bill to establish primary schools of agriculture in the Territories of the United States—to Committee on Agriculture (X)
"	"	HR14971	Apr. 11, 1904	" "	4668	A bill to establish a Bureau of Agricultural Education in the Department of Agriculture—to Committee on Agriculture (X)
"	3d	—				
59th	1st	HR16311	Mch. 7, 1906	Williams, of Miss.	3496 (Vol. No. 225)	A bill to incorporate the "Industrial Education League of the South" by John Sharp Williams (BX). This bill is carefully written and is based on progressive ideas
"	2d	HR24757	Jan. 22, 1907	Davis, of Minn.	1484, 1535, 2334, 4499 4500-2	A bill making annual appropriations for industrial education in agricultural high schools and in city high schools—10¢ per capita by States (contains a number of legislative principles later embodied in Smith-Hughes Act)
60th	1st	HR18204	Feb. 27, 1908	Davis, of Minn.	2628	A bill to provide appropriations for agricultural and industrial arts instruction in secondary schools and normal schools, etc.—to Committee on Agriculture (X)
"	"	Amendment	Mch. 10, 1908	Dolliver, of Iowa	3062	To amend the Annual Appropriations to U.S. Bureau of Education by providing $40,000 for special studies re industrial education, rural schools and mechanical colleges—to Committee on Appropriations (X)
"	"	S7005	May 7, 1908	Lodge, of Mass.	5846	A bill to incorporate the National Society for the Promotion of Industrial Education—to Committee on Judiciary (X)
"	2d	HR26737	Jan. 20, 1909	Davis, of Minn.	1196	A bill to cooperate with the states in encouraging instruction in farming and homemaking in agricultural secondary schools with branch experiment stations; instruction in non-agricultural industries and homemaking in city secondary schools; and in providing teachers for these *vocational subjects* in normal schools, and to appropriate money therefor and to regulate its expenditure—to Committee on Agriculture. (First use of "vocational" terminology) (X)

TABLE I. INDEX OF LEGISLATIVE REFERENCES—VOCATIONAL EDUCATION
(1900–1917)—*Continued*

(Compiled by J. C. Wright, June, 1947)

Congress	Session	Bills Introduced			Page References to Congressional Record	Title of Bill and Notes on Actions Taken by Congress (A) Referred to Committee on Education and Labor (B) Referred to Committee on Education (C) Referred to Committee on Agriculture and Forestry (X) No further action on Bill
		Bill No.	Date	By Whom		
61st	1st	S287	Mch. 22, 1909	Barkett, of Neb.	133	A bill for the advancement of instruction in agriculture, manual training and home economics in State Normal Schools (AX)
"	2d	HR10952	June 24, 1909	Davis, of Minn.	3786	A bill to cooperate with the States in encouraging instruction in agriculture, the trades and industries and home economics in secondary schools; in preparing teachers for those *vocational subjects* in State Normal Schools; and to appropriate money therefor and to regulate its expenditure (CX). Senator Page was very active in this and the 62d Cong. He co-operated with Smith of Ga. in the 63d. (Revision of HR10952)—to Committee on Agriculture (X)
"	"	S4675	Jan. 5, 1910	Dolliver, of Iowa	311 (Printed Hearings April 12, 13)	(Same as HR26737)—to Committee on Agriculture (X)
"	"	HR20374 S Doc 516	Feb. 8, 1910 Apr. 30, 1910	Davis, of Minn. Pres. of Senate	1622 5600	—to Committee on Agriculture (X) Presents a letter from Dr. Charles R. Richards, Pres. NSPIE, transmitting Report of a Committee on Industrial Education, memorializing Congress to make an appropriation to enable U.S. Bureau of Education to develop schools for industrial training (AX)
"	"	S8809	June 22, 1910	Dolliver, of Iowa	8713	(Same as HR10952) see Report No. 902 of Committee on Agriculture and Forestry. Bill includes extension departments in State colleges.
62d	1st	S3	Apr. 6, 1911	Page, of Vt.	100, 564, 2096, 2102, 2434, 3486, 4861, 5161–8, 7663–99, 7854, 8145, 8225, 9543–4, 10646–9, 10738, 10784–5, 10831, 11053, 11142, 11268–73, 11519–27, 11778.	A bill to cooperate with the states in encouraging instruction in agriculture, the trades and industries, and home economics in secondary schools; in maintaining instruction in these vocational subjects in State Normal Schools; in maintaining extension departments in State Colleges of Agriculture and Mechanic Arts; and to appropriate money and regulate its expenditure. (Defines secondary schools) (C) Report No. 405, with amendments, recommends that the bill does pass.
"	"	HR6333	Apr. 20, 1911	Davis, of Minn.	519	(Same as S3) (BX)
"	2d	HR15458	Dec. 12, 1911	Godwin, of N.C.	286	(Same as S3) (BX)
"	"	HR16842	Jan. 4, 1912	Anderson, of Ohio	677	(Same as S3) (BX)
"	"	HR18160 HR22871	Jan. 17, 1912 Apr. 4, 1912	Lever, of S.C. Lever, of S.C.	1052 (Later revised as HR22871)—4318, 4764, 9249, 9252, 10693, 10850–61, 11426–7, 11608–38, 11706–43, 11745, 11770	A bill to establish agricultural extension departments in connection with agricultural colleges in the several states receiving the benefits of an Act of Congress approved July 2, 1862, and Acts supplementary thereto—to Committee on Agriculture—Passed.
"	"	HR20476 S3	Feb. 20, 1912 Feb. 26, 1912	Goodwin, of Ark. Page, of Vt.	2273 2434	(Same as S3) (BX) S3 as amended by Committee on Agriculture and Forestry—see Senate Report No. 405
"	"	HR21490	Mch. 7, 1912	Wilson, of Pa.	2997	(Similar to S-3 in 1st Session plus teacher training in A. and M. Colleges)—to Committee on Agriculture
"	"	HR23581	Apr. 10, 1912	" " "	5081	Revision of HR12156 and HR21490 so as to conform closely to S-3 of Feb. 26, 1912—to Committee on Agriculture. Hearings held on April 23–26. (Page-Wilson bill)
"	"	Letter	Aug. 13, 1912	Davenport, of Ill.	10784	Criticizing Page bill S-3 as "dangerous to public schools"—placed in Record by Senator Page
"	"	S Doc 936	Aug. 17, 1912	Page, of Vt.	11142, 11631	Winslow Report on Industrial Education—sponsored by 19 "top" representatives of American Federation of Labor
"	3d	Speech Letters	Aug. 22, 1912 Jan. 27, 1913	Davis, of Minn. Page, of Vt.	11627 2096, 2102, 3025	Re need for industrial education Page inserts in the Congressional Record a number of letters re S-3.

Cong.	Sess.	No.	Date	Author	References	Notes
63d	1st	S3 / SJ Res. No. 5	Apr. 7, 1913 / " "	Page, of Vt. / Smith, of Ga.	46, 51, 3091, 5356 / 57, 1838–90, 2238–76, 4859, 5349–79, 5503, 5827	(Same as S–3 in previous Session) (CX) Senate Joint Resolution requesting President Wilson to appoint a Commission on National Aid to Vocational Education. The committee was appointed pursuant to Public Resolution No. 16, approved Jan. 20, 1914 (See H. Doc. 1004)
63d	1st	HR2874 / HR6932	Apr. 17, 1913 / July 18, 1913	Goodwin, of Ark. / Hobson, of Ala.	225, 7951 / 2545	(Same as HR20476 of 62d Congress) A bill to encourage, equalize and standardize vocational education among the states (BX)
"	"	S3091	Sept. 6, 1913	Smith, of Ga.	4330, 5478–10, 5662, 5843, 5928	A bill to provide for cooperative agricultural extension work between the agricultural colleges in the several states . . . and the U.S. Department of Agriculture (C)
"	"	HR7951	Sept. 6, 1913	Lever, of S.C.	4414	A bill to provide for cooperative agricultural extension work between the agricultural colleges in the several states receiving the benefits of an Act of Congress approved July 2, 1862, and of acts supplementary thereto, and the U.S. Department of Agriculture—to Committee on Agriculture. (Passed 2d Session)
"	2d	HR7951	Dec. 8, 1913	Lever, of S.C.	503, 1932–1947 (See original Index for additional reference)	Record reference contains full history of actions from introduction to approval by President.
"	"	Letter	Jan. 13, 1914	Redfield, of Mass.	1616	A letter re need for Federal aid to vocational education from William Redfield, Secretary of Commerce
"	"	HR16952	June 1, 1914	Hughes, of Ga.	9612	A bill to provide for the promotion of vocational education; to provide for cooperation with the states in the promotion of such education in agriculture and the trades and industries; to provide for cooperation with the states in the preparation of teachers of vocational subjects; and to appropriate money and regulate its expenditure (B)
"	"	S5706	" "	Smith, of Ga.	9503	(Same as above—and as recommended in following Report of Commission) (A)
"	"	H Doc. 1004	" "	Hughes, of Ga.	9537, 9611	"Report of Commission on National Aid to Vocational Education" in two volumes (B) and ordered to be printed—now a rare document. Volume One should be reprinted.
64th	1st	HR457 / S703	Dec. 6, 1915 / Dec. 7, 1915	Hughes, of Ga. / Smith, of Ga.	24, 92, 97, 1781, 6478–80, 9223–4, 11275, 11463–4, 11873–8	(Same as HR16952) (B) (Same as S5706) (A) Report No. 97—two pages—suggests full-time board
"	"	HR11250	Feb. 10, 1916	Hughes, of Ga.	2681, 3262, 3305, 3408, 3428, 3432, 4178, 6837, 7622, 9350, 11818	(Introduced as companion bill to S703) (B) Feb. 12, 1916, committed to Committee of the Whole House on the State of the Union and ordered to be printed
"	"	HR16971	July 13, 1916	Siegel, of N.Y.	1135, 2681, 4178, 5136, 6837, 7622, 9350	(Same as HR11250 plus inclusion of commercial education as part of trade and industrial education and funds for salaries of supervisors in all fields)
"	2d	Memorials favoring passage			3429	
"	"	H Con Res 75	Feb. 16, 1917	Oliver, of Ala.	3262, 3305, 3428, 3482, 3483, A415	House Joint Conference Resolution No. 75 on S–703—inserted in Sec. 5 "designate or create"
"	"	S Doc 711 / H Rept. 1495	— / —	Conferees Report / Conferees Report	1073, 3408, 3428–32	Passed by both Houses and signed by President Wilson February 23, 1917
"	"	Remarks	Feb. 19, 1917	Schall, of Minn.	Append. 415	A very good analysis of Smith-Hughes Act and of need for vocational education

this period the bills included provisions for "maintaining extension departments in state colleges of agriculture and mechanic arts" along with provisions for giving "instruction in agriculture, the trades and industries, and home economics." This mixture of function led to difficult problems in making provision for both state and federal administration. In 1912 a separate bill was drawn and introduced by Congressman Lever, of South Carolina, in which these conflicting purposes were avoided by limiting the bill to agriculture extension work. In 1914 the Smith-Lever Act became a law and the way was cleared for vocational education.

6. Finally the leaders, advocating federal aid for vocational education, concentrated on legislation requesting the President to appoint a Commission on National Aid to Vocational Education. This agitation led to the introduction by Senator Smith, of Georgia, of Senate Joint Resolution No. 5, on April 7, 1913. The commission was appointed early in 1914 and out.of its Report (published as House Document No. 1004, June 1, 1914), came the basic provisions later incorporated by Congress in the Smith-Hughes Act of February 23, 1917.

Legislative Developments, 1917–47. During the 30 years of progress under the Smith-Hughes Act from 1917 to 1947, there was only one Congress—the 75th—during which no new or supplementary legislative proposals relating to vocational education were introduced.

Over that thirty-year period a total of not less than 53 bills were before the two Houses—21 before the Senate and 32 before the House of Representatives. These measures were introduced by senators from seven different states and by members of the House of Representatives from sixteen different states, including the territories of Alaska and Hawaii and the Island of Puerto Rico.

Table II presents, chronologically, the story of legislation proposed and enacted, during the thirty-year period 1917–47, as supplementary to the Smith-Hughes Act. In some instances the same bill was reintroduced in subsequent sessions with or without the same number. To this extent they do not represent new proposals. Likewise, the custom prevailed of having companion bills in the House or Senate, as the case might be, thus increasing the number of bills but not the number of legislative proposals.

Students interested in reading the historical background of various pieces of legislation will find these charts a means of saving

TABLE II. INDEX OF LEGISLATIVE REFERENCES—VOCATIONAL EDUCATION (1917–1947)

(Compiled by J. C. Wright, June, 1947)

CONGRESS (1)	SESSION (2)	BILLS INTRODUCED — Bill No. (3)	Date (4)	By Whom (5)	PAGE REFERENCES TO CONGRESSIONAL RECORD (6)	TITLE OF BILL AND NOTES ON ACTIONS TAKEN BY CONGRESS (A) Referred to Committee on Education and Labor (B) Referred to Committee on Education (C) Referred to Committee on Agriculture and Forestry (X) No further action on Bill (7)
65th	2d	HR2455	June 15, 1917	Smith, of Ga.	3633 (First amendment by Congress)	An amendment to amend the Smith-Hughes Act of Feb. 23, 1917, to provide for temporary acceptance by the Governor and to authorize use of funds for printing, binding of law books—postage, etc. (A) Approved Oct. 6, 1917
"	"	HJ Res 277	Apr. 8, 1918	Kalanianaola, of T.H.	4821	A resolution to extend the benefits of the Smith-Hughes Act to Hawaii
66th	1st	HR11442	Jan. 5, 1920	Green, of Iowa	1078	A bill to amend the Smith-Hughes Act with respect to the composition of the Board (BX)
"	2d	HR11724	Jan. 13, 1920	" " "	1518	(Same as above as amended)
"	"	S4133				
"	3d	—	Mch. 25, 1920	Kenyon, of Iowa	4802	(Same as Green bills) (AX)
67th	1st	HR21	Apr. 11, 1921	Fess, of Ohio	87	A bill to amend the Smith-Hughes Act by extending its benefits to Hawaii (BX)
"	"	S1061	Apr. 21, 1921	Kenyon, of Iowa	526, 4095 1782, 1890, 2036, 2355, 2428	(Same as above) (AX)
"	"	HR6611	May 25, 1921	Sweet, of Iowa	In Senate 4094–97, Conferees Rep't—4471–76, 4485, 4557–63	A bill to create a Veterans Bureau. In connection therewith there was much discussion of the need for a Federal Board for Vocational Education after the Rehabilitation program was transferred to new Bureau and Senate passed bill with Board abolished. It was caught in House and conferees eliminated "joker" clause after much hard work. (Amend. No. 13, p. 4558, Vol. 401)
"	2d	—				
"	3d	—				
"	4th	HR13769	Jan. 11, 1923	Baldwin, of Hawaii	1617	A bill to amend Smith-Hughes Act so as to extend its benefits to the Territory of Hawaii (BX)
68th	1st	S1408	Dec. 17, 1923	Fess, of Ohio	321 476, 567, 1225, 1267, 1550, 3248–9, 3599–0, 3778, 4000	A bill to amend the Smith-Hughes Act (AX)
"	"	HR4727	Dec. 20, 1923	Jarret, of Hawaii		A bill to extend the provisions of certain laws to the Territory of Hawaii (B) Passed and approved March 10, 1924
"	2d	HR6161	Jan. 24, 1924	Davila, of P.R.	1431	A bill to amend the Smith-Hughes Act so as to extend its benefits to The Island of Puerto Rico (BX)
69th	1st	—				
"	2d	—				
70th	1st	S1731	Dec. 15, 1927	George, of Ga.	677, 3910, 6083–6218, 8779	A bill to provide for the further development of vocational education in the several states and territories (C). Passed and approved Feb. 5, 1929— (George-Reed Act)

TABLE II. INDEX OF LEGISLATIVE REFERENCES—VOCATIONAL EDUCATION (1917–1947)—Continued

(Compiled by J. C. Wright, June, 1947)

		Bills Introduced			Page References to Congressional Record	Title of Bill and Notes on Actions Taken by Congress (A) Referred to Committee on Education and Labor (B) Referred to Committee on Education (C) Referred to Committee on Agriculture and Forestry (X) No further action on Bill
Congress	Session	Bill No.	Date	By Whom		
(1)	(2)	(3)	(4)	(5)	(6)	(7)
70th	1st	HR9201 HR12241	Jan. 12, 1928 Mch. 20, 1928	Menges, of Pa. Reed, of N.Y.	1417 5088, 5708, 6702, 7987, 2375, 2376–93, 2406–76, and 2909	(Same as S1731) (B). Passed as S1731 in House
"	2d	HR15211	Dec. 11, 1928	Reed, of N.Y.	434, 1706, 2780	A bill to amend Sec. 7 of Smith-Hughes Act so as to authorize "necessary funds" for administration (BX)
71st	1st	S2113	Nov. 14, 1929	Smith, of S.C.	5532	A bill to aid in effectuating the purposes of the Federal laws for the promotion of vocational agriculture (CX)
"	2d	HR10250	Feb. 25, 1930	Reed, of N.Y.	4249 (FFA National Charter)	A bill to aid in effectuating the purpose of Federal laws for the promotion of vocational agriculture (BX)
"	"	S2113	Feb. 26, 1930	Smith, of S.C.	4254 (FFA National Charter)	Report of Committee on Agriculture and Forestry—favorable, No. 227
"	"	HR10821 S3969 Letter	Mch. 17, 1930 Mch. 19, 1930 May 24, 1930	Reed, of N.Y. Capper, of Kan. J. C. Wright	5472 5567 9491	A bill to provide for the further development of vocational education (BX) (Same as HR10821) (AX) Commending address by Representative Ayres on "Scientific Adult Education"
"	3d	S5139	Dec. 8, 1930	Bingham, of Conn.	296, 2123, 3179, 4466, 5251, 5341, 7261	A bill to extend the provisions of certain laws relating to vocational education to Puerto Rico.
"	"	HR12901	Dec. 8, 1930	Reed, of N.Y.	368, 6272, 6417, 6640, 6800, 6705, 7285	A bill to extend the provisions of certain laws relating to vocational education to Puerto Rico
"	"	S2113 S3969	Jan. 21, 1931 Feb. 26, 1931	Smith, of S.C. Capper, of Kan.	2601 6038, 6963 (Com. Report No. 1793)	(Same bill carried over) (CX) Same bill passed
72d	1st	HR8241 S3884 Economy Discussion	Jan. 22, 1932 Mch. 1, 1932	Patterson, of Ala. Capper, of Kan. (General)	2561 4987 8179, 8319, 8446, 8517, 8620–1, 8803, 9006, 9234, 9271, 9786	A bill for the further development of vocational education (BX) (Same as above) (AX) Led by Hon. Lewis Douglas of Ariz., there were numerous attempts to curtail appropriations for vocational education. Championed by Reed of New York, LaGuardia, of New York, and a number of Southern Congressmen, the issue was won and the program continued through the crisis of the early 30's
"	2d	Remarks	—	(General)	1402, 1439, 1718, 3458, 3579	The Economy discussion extended
73d	1st	Report	May 30, 1933	LaFollette, of Wis.	4579–80	"Committee of 20" submitted its Report to Citizens Conference on May 5, 1933. It was adopted and on May 30 Mr. LaFollette asked permission to have it printed in the Record—request granted. Subject of Report— "Vocational Education and Problems of Reconstruction"—

The President discusses his policy re vocational education over the radio; a bill history table:

Cong.	Sess.	Bill No.	Date	Source / Sponsor	Document Nos.	Remarks
	"	Radio	June 13, 1933	Pres. Roosevelt	5958-60	The President discusses his policy re vocational education over the radio
	2d	S2119	Jan. 10, 1934	George, of Ga.	304, 7599, 7885, 8483, 9375	A bill to provide for the further development of vocational education (C) Passed
	"	HR7059	Jan. 18, 1934	Ellzey, of Miss.	907, 3634, 5272, 7371, 7462-3, 7477	(Same as above) (B). Passed as George-Ellzey Act. Approved May 21, 1934
	"	HR7089	Jan. 19, 1934	Jeffers, of Ala.	950	(Same as above) (BX)
	"	HR7802	Feb. 8, 1934	Black, of Ala.	2230	(Same as above) (BX)
74th	1st	HR8024	May 18, 1935	King, of Hawaii	7429	A bill to authorize the Secretary of War to dispose of material no longer needed by the Army—to the Committee on Military Affairs
	"	S2883	May 22, 1935	George, of Ga.	7964, 9258	A bill to provide for the further development of vocational education (CX)
	"	HR8188	May 23, 1935	Dimond, of Alaska	8118	A bill to extend vocational education to Alaska (BX)
74th	1st	HR8211	May 24, 1935	Disney, of Okla.	8213	(Same as S2883) (BX)
	"	S3167	June 27, 1935	Schwellenbach, of Wash.	10242	(Same as S2883) (AX)
	"	HR8809	July 10, 1935	Lee, of Okla.	10995	(Same as S2883) (AX)
	2d	S2883	(over)	George, of Ga.	2278, 2434, 4394, 6031, 6171, 6267, 6273, 6275, 6076	S2883 was carried over from the 1st Session and passed
	"	HR8024	Jan. 10, 1936	King, of Hawaii	728, 782, 2016, 2443, 2588, 2591, 2610	(Same as HR8024 of 1st Session)
	"	HR10190	Jan. 14, 1936	Deen, of Ga.	411, 7962, 7978	A bill to provide for the further development of vocational education (BX)
	"	HR11328	Feb. 20, 1936	Lee, of Okla.	2534	(Same as above) (BX)
	"	HR12120	Apr. 1, 1936	Deen, of Ga.	4769, 5040, 7955-60, 7963-78, 7978, 8009-10, 8202-3, 8351, 8363, 9568	HR10160 replaced by a revised bill —(B). Passed approved June 8, 1936
	"	S3167	(over)	Schwellenbach, of Wash.	4367, 4488, 4766	Further discussion of this bill introduced in 1st Session.
	"	Letter	June 16, 1936	Pres. Roosevelt	9648 (Letter to Cong. Deen)	President Roosevelt writes that he signed the bill reluctantly, and that he proposed to appoint a group to study the subject of vocational education. An Advisory Committee of 24 members was appointed September 19, 1936. Its scope was enlarged on April 19, 1937, to include general education—Floyd Reeves, Chairman
75th	1st	Petitions, Remarks, and Telegrams re Need			1467, 4541-3, 4849, 4856, 4979-83, 6396, 6403	As a result of the pressure brought on Congress to pass the George-Deen Act, an avalanche of telegrams, letters and petitions came in. Many were critical of delaying attitude of the Administration—World War II only three years ahead!
	"	HR7277 / Rept. No. 945	May 27, 1937	Fitzgerald of Connecticut	3277, 5096, 5400 / 6631-6641, 6646	To enable the Department of Labor to formulate and promote the furtherance of labor standards necessary to safeguard the welfare of apprentices and to cooperate with the states in the promotion of such standards. (First introduced in May, 1937, as HR6205. See p. 3277.)
		S. Rept. 1076 / Approved / —	Aug. 20, 1937	Comm. on Educ. and Labor / President	8163, 8489, 8505-6 / 8581, 8664, 8729 / 9457 (Pub. No. 308)	
	2d / 3d	Remarks	Feb. 25, 1938	Cochrane, of Mo.	2479	Cong. Cochrane criticizes Report of "Advisory Committee on Education" —(Reeves Committee)
76th	1st	HR6157	May 4, 1939	Larabee, of Ind.	5153	A bill to amend the Smith-Hughes Act (BX)

TABLE II. INDEX OF LEGISLATIVE REFERENCES—VOCATIONAL EDUCATION (1917–1947)

(Compiled by J. C. Wright, June, 1947)

| CONGRESS (1) | SESSION (2) | BILLS INTRODUCED | | | PAGE REFERENCES TO CONGRESSIONAL RECORD (6) | TITLE OF BILL AND NOTES ON ACTIONS TAKEN BY CONGRESS (A) Referred to Committee on Education and Labor (B) Referred to Committee on Education (C) Referred to Committee on Agriculture and Forestry (X) No further action on Bill (7) |
		Bill No. (3)	Date (4)	By Whom (5)		
76th	1st	S2460	May 19, 1939	George, of Ga.	5773	A bill relating to the development of vocational education in the several states and proposing drastic revisions requested by organized labor—(AX)
"	2d	S3170	Jan. 23, 1940	Murray, of Mont.	539	A bill for vocational guidance and training of youth 16–25, etc. (AX)
"	3d	HR8313	Feb. 6, 1940	Marcantonio, of N.Y.	1040	" " " " " " (BX)
"	"	HR8324	Feb. 6, 1940	Geyer, of Calif.	1129	" " " " " " (BX)
77th	1st	Remarks	Dec. 4, 1941	Davis, of Pa.	9411, 9412	Senator James J. Davis inserts in Record statement by J. C. Wright on "Vocational Education and Post War Problems"
"	2d	—				
78th	1st	S1946	May 23, 1944	George, of Ga.	4844	A bill to provide vocational training and retraining, etc.—Co-sponsors: Thomas, of Utah; Hill, of Ala.; Aiken, of Vt.; LaFollette, of Wis.; and Ellender, of La. (AX)
"	2d	HR5079	June 22, 1944	Dondero, of Mich.	6456	A bill to provide vocational training and retraining, etc. (BX)
79th	1st	S619	Feb. 26, 1945	George, of Ga.	1410	A bill to provide—(same as S1946) (A)
"	"	S1080	June 1, 1945	Thomas, of Utah	5385, 6123, 6128, 6407	A bill to amend the Smith-Hughes Act so as to provide that "administrators, directors, supervisors, and teachers shall be appointed in accordance with the laws of the respective States." (A) (Passed. Lost in House.)
"	"	HR3421	June 8, 1945	Flanagan, of Va.	5837	(Same as above) (BX)
"	"	HR4384	Oct. 17, 1945	Barden, of N.C.	9726	A bill to amend the Act of June 8, 1936, relating to vocational education, so as to provide for the further development of vocational education in the several states and territories. (B) (Passed and approved Aug. 1, 1946)
"	2d	S619	June 26, 1946	George, of Ga.	7663, 8453–5, 8559, 10372, 10555, 10638, 10733 A4014 (Appendix Volume)	Discussion Senate Report No. 1588 favoring passage with suggested amendments—passed and sent to House
"	"	Statement H Rep't 2658	June 29, 1946	Johnson, of Texas	9990, 10349–50	Re HR4384 Barden, of N.C., presents HR Report No. 2658 by the Committee on Education re S619 which was referred to the Committee of the Whole House on the State of the Union
"	"		July 24, 1946	Barden, of N.C.		
"	"	Signed	Aug. 1, 1946	President Truman	10758	After the Conferees had agreed on differences in the Senate and House bills both Houses accepted HR4384, as amended, and sent it to the President for approval. It was signed on Aug. 1, 1946, in the presence of Senator George, of Ga.; Cong. Barden, of N.C.; Senator Hill, of Ala.; Senator Johnston, of S.C.; Mr. and Mrs. L. H. Dennis; Mr. and Mrs. Charles W. Sylvester; Mr. and Mrs. M. D. Mobley; Mr. C. L. Greiber; Mr. Ira W. Kibby; Dr. John W. Studebaker, and Dr. J. C. Wright

time in looking up important page references. Where bound copies of the *Congressional Record* are available at local libraries, the page references in column (6) will make for quick reading when the appropriate volume for the Congress and session has been secured.

AMENDMENTS TO THE SMITH-HUGHES ACT

The time-honored procedure of making changes in existing law has been for the legislative body to enact new legislation amending the law by adding new provisions or by modifying or repealing provisions already in the law. When this procedure is followed, a bill is drawn up, introduced in one of the Houses of Congress, and the same legislative steps are followed as for original legislation. Under another procedure the Congress authorizes the President to accomplish the same purpose by executive order.

During the administration of President Hoover, Congress passed a Reorganization Act under which the President was given authority to reorganize agencies of the government through consolidations, transfer, and abolition of functions thereof. Certain agencies were excepted, but, for others, executive orders of the President directed toward these ends were subject only to veto by the Congress.

During his administration President Franklin D. Roosevelt was given similar authority. The same procedure was followed in 1946 when President Truman issued his plan for reorganizing various agencies of the Government.

Amending the Act by Legislative Enactment. Public No. 64, 65th Congress, approved October 6, 1917, was passed by Congress at the request of the Federal Board for Vocational Education in order to correct an oversight in the basic Act. Apparently the framers of this legislation did not know that under a general law (30 U.S. Statute 316) specific authorization must be included in federal legislation if funds are to be used for the purchase of periodicals and books of reference. Also, under a similar law (28 U.S. Statute 622), specific authorization must be included in federal legislation if funds are to be used for printing and binding, and for postage on foreign mail.

In addition to these authorizations, the first amendment recognized that the inauguration of the vocational program in many of the states would be delayed one to four years if the states had to wait on their legislatures to meet in regular session and pass their acceptance acts. For example, at that time the legislature in Alabama met regularly once each four years. The only alternative was for the states to go to the expense of calling a special session. Both the delay and the expense of a special session were avoided by this amendment through a proclamation of the governor. The amendment reads as follows:

> In any state the legislature of which met in nineteen hundred and seventeen and failed for any reason to accept the provisions of the Vocational Education Act, as provided in section five of said Act, if the governor of that state, so far as he is authorized to do so shall accept the provisions of said Act and designate or create a state board of not less than three members to act in cooperation with the Federal Board for Vocational Education and shall designate the state treasurer as custodian for all moneys allotted to that state under said Act, the Federal Board shall, if such legislature took no adverse action on the acceptance of said Act in nineteen hundred and seventeen, recognize such state board for the purposes of said Act until the legislature of that state meets in regular session in due course and has been in session sixty days.

The second amendment was a part of general legislation passed in 1935 which provided that certain permanent appropriations should be subject to annual consideration and appropriation by Congress. In the case of the Smith-Hughes Act, it continued the permanent appropriations to the states provided in Sections 1, 2, 3, and 4, but changed the administrative appropriations in Section 7 to an annual authorization.

The general law provides:

> Section 2. (2) Effective July 1, 1935, the permanent appropriations under the appropriation titles listed in subsection (b) of this section are repealed, and such portions of any acts as make permanent appropriations to be expended under such accounts are amended so as to authorize, in lieu thereof, annual appropriations from the general funds of the Treasury in identical terms and in such amounts as now provided by the laws providing such permanent appropriations. . . ."

Subsection (*b*) of Section 2 included as Item *22* the following language:

> (22) Salaries and expenses, Federal Board for Vocational Education (fiscal year) (0—801).

Neither of these two amendments changed or repealed in any way the basic provisions of the Smith-Hughes Act.[3]

---

[3] Extracts from Public No. 473, 73d Congress, H.R. 9410.

Amending the Act by Executive Order. 1. Under the Reorganization Act of June 30, 1932, President Hoover included the following proposal:

> It is proposed to transfer the powers and duties of the Federal Board for Vocational Education to the Department of the Interior, and it is recommended that legislation be enacted abolishing the Board. Pending such legislation, the Board will serve in an advisory capacity to the Secretary of the Interior.

The executive orders were issued on December 9, 1932, to become effective 61 days later. However, Congress vetoed the portion of the Order transferring the Federal Board for Vocational Education.

2. Shortly before the close of the 72d Congress, President Roosevelt issued Executive Order No. 6166, dated June 10, 1933. By this Order he changed the Federal Board for Vocational Education from an administrative board to an advisory board. The portion of the executive order relating to vocational education reads as follows:

> Section 15. *Vocational Education.* The functions of the Federal Board for Vocational Education are transferred to the Department of the Interior, and the Board shall act in an advisory capacity without compensation.

Under the provisions of the Order it was to become effective 61 days from its date. However, as the effective date of August 10 approached, the Order was amended so that transfer of the functions was postponed 60 days to October 10, 1933. On this date it became effective.

3. Under the Reorganization Act of 1939 the U.S. Office of Education, including the Federal Board for Vocational Education in its advisory capacity, was transferred from the Interior Department to the Federal Security Agency on July 1, 1939.

4. On May 16, 1946, President Truman promulgated his Reorganization Plan No. 2 which related to Education and Welfare. The following provision was included:

> Section 8. *Federal Board for Vocational Education:* The Federal Board for Vocational Education and all its functions are abolished.

It can be said that the basic Act has been amended twice by Congress and three times by executive order, with the consent of

Congress. However, none of these amendments affected the fundamental purposes of the Act or the cooperative relationships between the federal and state governments.

Legislation Coming After the Smith-Hughes Act. In the thirty years covered by Tables I and II there have been twelve supplementary and related acts passed by Congress. The following chronological list includes a brief description of the purpose of each act and information as to its present status:

Smith-Sears Vocational Rehabilitation Act.[4] Congress passed legislation on behalf of disabled veterans as follows:

> An Act to provide for Vocational Rehabilitation and return to civil employment of disabled persons discharged from the military or naval forces of the United States, and for other purposes. Approved June 27, 1918.

The United States, like the other nations in World War I, decided to rehabilitate and re-educate its disabled soldiers and sailors who by reason of service were unable to resume their former occupations.

Vocational Rehabilitation of the Disabled. An act[5] that was passed at the close of the 66th Congress and approved by the President on June 2, 1920, provided "for the promotion of vocational rehabilitation of persons disabled in industry or otherwise, and their return to civil employment."

Provisions of Smith-Hughes Act for Hawaii. On April 8, 1918, the Hawaiian delegate, Mr. Kalanianaole, introduced into the 65th Congress, 2d Session, House Joint Res. 277, in the House of Representatives. This joint resolution was intended to extend to the Territory of Hawaii the same right that is given to the states to participate in the funds for vocational education appropriated under the Smith-Hughes Act.

The Resolution was brought before the Federal Board at its meeting on June 6, and the Board voted to approve all legislation originating in Congress extending the provisions of the Smith-Hughes Act in the manner provided for the states to Alaska, Hawaii, and Puerto Rico. Apparently the joint resolution failed to secure the necessary attention in Congress and was not passed.

In May, 1923, Mr. Raymond C. Brown, Secretary of State of

---

[4] Public No. 178, 65th Congress, S. 4557.
[5] Public No. 236, 66th Congress, H.R. 4438.

Hawaii, called on the director of the Federal Board for Vocational Education to request that the Board make a study of the needs for vocational education in Hawaii.

However, it was not possible for representatives of the Federal Board to go to Hawaii before a year had passed and, in the interim, Governor Farrington came to Washington and promoted legislation in Congress extending the benefits of vocational education to Hawaii. This Act was approved on March 10, 1924, as Section 4 of Public No. 35, 64th Congress. The Act authorized an annual appropriation of $30,000 to be available under the same conditions as moneys appropriated to the states by the Smith-Hughes Act.

George-Reed Act of 1929. After ten years of progress, under the funds available through the Smith-Hughes Act, agricultural and home economics leaders joined together and urged Congress to enact new legislation which would increase the amount of federal aid to the states for these two services. On December 15, 1927, Senator George, of Georgia, introduced S. 1731, "A bill to provide for the further development of vocational education in the several states and territories." On March 20, 1928, Congressman Reed, of New York, introduced a companion bill in the House. These two measures were given the usual hearings and discussions over a period of one year, and passed as S. 1731. The Act was signed by President Coolidge, February 5, 1929.

Provisions of Smith-Hughes Act for Puerto Rico. Puerto Rico had made several attempts to have benefits of the Smith-Hughes Act extended to the Island before Theodore Roosevelt, Jr., became its governor, but none of them had been successful.

In 1930, Governor Roosevelt asked the Federal Board for assistance in making a survey of the need for a program of vocational education. The Board authorized its director and its chief of the trade and industrial service to make the study. As a result of this study, Congress passed S. 5139, "A bill to extend the provisions of certain laws relating to vocational education and civilian rehabilitation to Puerto Rico." The Act was approved March 3, 1931.

The Acceptance Act designated the insular treasurer as custodian of federal moneys, created an Insular Board for Vocational Education to cooperate with the Federal Board, and appropriated funds for matching federal money and for administrative expenses.

The Insular Board for Vocational Education is an ex officio board of three members—the Commissioner of Education as chairman and executive officer, the Commissioner of Agriculture and Industry, and the Commissioner of Labor.

George-Ellzey Act, 1934. In the midst of the depression, the five-year period for which the George-Reed Act provided drew to a close. Again the leaders in vocational education acting through the American Vocational Association, approached their friends in Congress. On January 10, 1934, Senator George introduced S. 2119, "A bill to provide for the further development of vocational education in the several states and territories."

On January 18, Congressman Ellzey, of Mississippi, introduced a companion bill (H.R. 7059) in the House. The House bill was followed by two additional bills, one introduced by Congressman Jeffers, of Alabama, and the other by his colleague, Congressman Black, who became a Justice of the United States Supreme Court in 1937. The bill passed the House and the Senate and was approved by President Roosevelt, May 21, 1934. An analysis of its provisions are given in Table II.

Disposal of Surplus Equipment. In order to enable the War Department to dispose of surplus equipment which could be used for vocational training, the 74th Congress passed H.R. 8024, "A bill to authorize the Secretary of War to dispose of material no longer needed by the Army. The Act was approved by President Roosevelt on February 28, 1936, and provides that:

> The Secretary of War be, and he is hereby, authorized in his discretion to dispose of, without charge, except for costs of transportation, handling, and packing, to such schools as he may select, for use in courses of vocational training and instruction, such machinery, mechanical equipment, and tools as may be obsolete or no longer needed by the Army.

George-Deen Act of 1936. During the middle 30's the public schools needed further extension of their vocational programs in all fields and in certain new fields for which no funds had been available. Again the American Vocational Association took the lead in presenting these needs to Congress. As early as May 22, 1935— or two years before the expiration of the George-Ellzey Act— Senator George of Georgia introduced S. 2883, "A bill to provide for the further development of vocational education in the several states and territories." The bill was referred to the Committee on Agriculture and Forestry.

A number of House bills were introduced. The sponsors of these bills included Congressman Disney, of Oklahoma; Schwellenbach, of Washington; Lee, of Oklahoma; and Deen, of Georgia. After the usual hearings and debates, Congress passed H.R. 12120, a bill introduced by Congressman Deen of Georgia and having the same title as S. 2883. The Act was approved by President Roosevelt on June 8, 1936. In a letter to Congressman Deen, the President wrote that he signed the bill reluctantly, and that he proposed to appoint a group to study the subject of vocational education. Acting on this commitment he later appointed an "Advisory Committee" of 24 members in September, 1936. Dr. Floyd Reeves was chairman of the Committee. An analysis of the provisions of the George-Deen Act is given in Table II.

An Act Authorizing the Sale of Scrap Metals. Many vocational schools do not know of the Act approved June 15, 1938, which authorizes the Secretary of the Navy to sell surplus scrap metals to certain institutions of learning. This Act provides that:

> . . . the Secretary of the Navy is authorized, in his discretion, to sell, at the prices established for issue to naval activities, surplus scrap metals of the Navy, to schools, colleges, and universities for use in courses of instruction in vocational training: *Provided further*, That any costs incident to the transportation or delivery of such scrap metals shall be charged to the purchaser.

Acts Relating to War Training—World War II. As the war began to spread over the entire world in 1939 and 1940, it became evident that the United States would be brought into the conflict. Late in the spring of 1940, the Bureau of the Budget, at the request of the President, asked the Office of Education to submit budget estimates for a program of vocational education to train war-production workers. When the estimates were submitted to the Bureau of the Budget, the President recommended an appropriation and Congress enacted the necessary legislation to inaugurate the program.

The Act approved on June 27, 1940, was followed by a number of other acts providing additional funds for vocational training for war-production workers.

Reconversion Act, 1944. "To aid in the reconversion from a war to a peace economy through the distribution of Government surplus property and to establish a Surplus Property Board to effectuate the same, and for other purposes," P.L. 457, approved October 3, 1944, made provision in Section 13 for the disposal of surplus property to states, their political divisions, and various instrumentalities where such disposal would be in the public interest.

The following paragraph in Section 13 contains specific provisions for the participation of trade and industrial schools along with all other public and nonprofit educational institutions:

> (1) (A) Surplus property that is appropriate for school, classroom, or other educational use may be sold or leased to the states and their political subdivisions and instrumentalities, and tax-supported educational institutions, and to other nonprofit educational institutions which have been held exempt from taxation under Section 101 (6) of the Internal Revenue Code.

George-Barden Act, 1946. The Senate and House bills leading up to the George-Barden Act were before Congress for a period of two years before the law was enacted. On May 23, 1944, Senator George, of Georgia, with six co-sponsors, introduced S. 1946 in the 78th Congress. The following February he again introduced the measure as S. 619 in the 79th Congress, 1st Session.

On October 17, 1945, Congressman Barden, of North Carolina, introduced H.R. 4384, "A bill to amend the George-Deen Act." The Senate passed S. 619 and the House amended it by substituting the language of its own bill and asked for conferees. In its revised form S. 619 was passed and signed by President Truman on August 1, 1946.

AN ANALYSIS OF THE GEORGE-BARDEN ACT[7]

Public Law 586 amends the George-Deen Act of 1936, designed "to provide for the further development of vocational education in the several states and territories." In the 1947 revision of the *Statement of Policies*, Bulletin No. 1., the U.S. Office of Education says, "The chief characteristic of the George-Barden Act as contrasted with previous vocational education legislation is flexibility. Some of the specific limitations on the use of funds were omitted from this Act and provisions were included to allow for new phases of work." It might well have been added that certain activities which previously developed under administrative approval were given legislative status under this Act, for example, supervision of the activities of the Future Farmers of America and the New Farmers of America, by teachers of agriculture, and the providing of training programs for apprentices.

---

[7] Public Law 586, 79th Congress, 2d Session, S. 619.

The most important respects in which the George-Barden Act differs from the Smith-Hughes and George-Deen Acts are:

1. The George-Barden Act provides one appropriation for each of the four service fields and no separate appropriation for teacher training. This same procedure was followed in the case of distributive education in the George-Deen Act. A state makes its own determination of the proportion of the allotment in a given field to be used for teacher training.

2. Federal funds under the George-Barden Act may be used for *maintenance* of administration and supervision. Under the George-Deen Act federal funds could not be used for administration and only for salaries and expenses in supervision. The Smith-Hughes Act allows for salaries of supervisors of agriculture only.

3. Under the George-Barden Act federal funds may be used for purchase or rent of equipment and supplies for vocational instruction. Section 17 of the Smith-Hughes Act concludes with the sentence, "No portion of any moneys appropriated under this Act for the benefit of the states shall be applied directly or indirectly, to the purchase, erection, preservation, or repair of any building (or buildings) or equipment."

4. The George-Barden Act, in Section 7, and the George-Deen Act, in Section 6, provide that "the appropriations made under authority of this Act shall be subject to the same conditions and limitations as the appropriations made to carry out the Smith-Hughes Act; except that . . . ," and here four exceptions almost identical in the two Acts follow. The George-Barden Act adds a fifth exception, namely, "pre-employment schools and classes organized for persons over eighteen years of age or who have left the full-time school may be operated for less than nine months per year and less than thirty hours per week and without the requirement that a minimum of 50 per centum of the time must be given to shop work on a useful or productive basis." Section 11 of the Smith-Hughes Act says that "such schools or classes giving instruction to persons who have not entered upon employment shall require that at least half of the time of such instruction be given to practical work on a useful or productive basis, such instruction to extend over not less than nine months per year and not less than thirty hours per week."

The U.S. Office of Education has set up a third classification of all-day trade school—namely, Type C—to designate schools or classes to be operated under this provision of the George-Barden Act.

The following paragraphs present a brief analysis of the Act.

Section 1. Cites the Act as the "Vocational Education Act of 1946."

Section 2. Defines *states and territories, state plan, state board,* and *Smith-Hughes Vocational Education Act.*

Section 3. *a*) Authorizes appropriations for:

(1) Vocational education in agriculture, $10,000,000

(2) Vocational education in home economics, 8,000,000

(3) Vocational education in trades and industries, 8,000,000

(4) Vocational education in distributive occupations, 2,500,000

b) Funds may be used for *purposes specified* in subsection (*a*), paragraphs (1) to (4):

—in maintenance of adequate programs of administration, supervision, and teacher training.

—for salaries and necessary travel expenses of teachers, teacher trainers, vocational counselors, supervisors, and directors of vocational education and vocational guidance.

—for securing necessary educational information and data as a basis for the proper development of programs of vocational education and vocational guidance.

—for training and work-experience training programs for out-of-school youths.

—for training programs for apprentices.

—for purchase or rent of equipment and supplies for vocational instruction.

Section 4. One hundred per cent matching.

Section 5. Payments to states semiannually.

Section 6. Salary and travel of state director prorated.

Section 7. Same conditions and limitations as Smith-Hughes Act.

Exceptions:

1. Home economics subject to same requirements as agriculture in the Smith-Hughes Act, except for six months supervised practice.

2. Trade and industrial part-time schools may be operated less than 144 hours per year.

3. Required one-third of trade and industrial funds for part-time schools may include any part-time day school or evening school for workers over 16 years of age.

4. Distributive education restricted to part-time and evening classes.

5. Requirements of the trade and industrial day school may be modified for persons over 18 years of age or for those who have left the full-time school.

6. Use of administrative funds by the Office of Education.

Section 8. *a*) Appropriations may not be used for any but bona fide vocational training in industrial plants.

b) After June 30, 1951, not more than 10 per cent of a fund may be used for equipment.

Section 9. Authorizes appropriation of $350,000 annually for administration of vocational education by the Office of Education. Approved August 1, 1946.

Appropriations for fiscal year 1947 had been made under authorization of the George-Deen Act before the above amendment was approved. Therefore, payments to the states were made in terms of the unamended Act. The first allotments to the states under the terms and conditions of the amendment and the revised state plans were for fiscal year 1948.

Whatever else may have been read into these various vocational education acts in regard to the relationship between the Federal Government and the states the facts are:

1. Participation on the part of a state is entirely voluntary.

2. The amount of money to which a state may be entitled is fixed by a population ratio.

3. A state plan is the contractual agreement of operation.

4. When a state violates the contract, the only penalty is the withholding of allotments.

5. The only redress open to the state is an appeal to Congress through the state board.

The *Statement of Policies for the Administration of Vocational Education* (known as Bulletin No. 1), issued in 1917 and revised 1922, 1926, 1937, and 1947, is the official interpretation of these vocational education acts. In it will be found the answer to many questions which naturally arise concerning the meaning of the acts themselves.

CHAPTER IX

Federal Legislation For Vocational - Technical Education (1947-1961)

The federal government indicated its continuous concern for the implementation of vocational education programs during the 80th through the 87th Sessions of Congress, covering the period 1947-1961. During this 15 year period, a number of bills relating to vocational education were introduced. Eleven public laws directly affecting programs of vocational education were enacted.

Federal legislation involving or pertaining to vocational education falls in two categories: (1) That administered by the U. S. Office of Education and State Boards for Vocational Education; and (2) that administered by other federal and/or state agencies. The following descriptions of federal legislation fall in the first of these categories.

Some aspects of training carried on under federal acts administered by the Department of Agriculture, the Department of Interior, and the Department of Defense may be classified as vocational education, but fall in the second category and so are not included here.

GEORGE-BARDEN ACT EXTENDED TO VIRGIN ISLANDS[1]

This act extended the benefits of the Vocational Education Act of 1946 to the Virgin Islands, and authorized an annual appropriation of $40,000. The legislation was introduced at the request of the Department of Interior following conferences with the Division of Vocational Education. A significant provision of the act was that the Commissioner of Education, with the approval of the Federal Security Administrator (now Secretary of Health, Education, and Welfare) could modify the apportionment of funds among the various fields of vocational education to meet existing conditions in the Virgin Islands.

---

[1] Public Law 81–462, 81st Congress, 2nd Session, S. 493; approved March 18, 1950.

FUTURE FARMERS OF AMERICA RECOGNIZED BY CONGRESS[2]

The purposes of this act were to incorporate the Future Farmers of America, a National organization of vocational agriculture students, and to clarify the relationships between the organization and the U. S. Office of Education.

Major provisions of the act were designation of the powers of the corporation; establishment of the headquarters and the principal offices of the corporation in the District of Columbia; definition of eligibility for membership in the corporation and the rights and privileges of members; provision for national student officers of the corporation and a board of directors composed of the Chief of the Agricultural Education Branch, four staff members of the Agricultural Education Branch, and four state supervisors of agricultural education; designation of tenure of office and meetings; and exclusive rights to the use of the name of Future Farmers of America, the initials FFA, and the adopted emblem of the organization.

GEORGE-BARDEN ACT EXTENDED TO GUAM[3]

The extension of the benefits of the Vocational Education Act of 1946 to Guam and authorization of an annual appropriation of $80,000 were the major purposes of this act. The same provision was included with respect to use of funds without regard to fields of vocational education, as stipulated in the Virgin Islands Bill, Public Law 462, of the 81st Congress.

TITLE II OF GEORGE-BARDEN ACT. VOCATIONAL EDUCATION IN PRACTICAL NURSE TRAINING[4]

This legislation is known as the "Health Amendments Act of 1956." It provided for the amendment of the Vocational Education Act of 1946 to include a Title II, "Vocational Education in Practical Nurse training." The funds appropriated under this act were to be used "to extend and improve practical nurse training. . . ."

---

[2] Public Law 81–740, 81st Congress, 2nd Session, S. 2868; approved August 30, 1950.

[3] Public Law 84–896, 84th Congress, 2nd Session, H.R. 11522; approved August 1, 1956.

[4] Public Law 84–911, 84th Congress, 2nd Session, S. 3958; approved August 2, 1956.

The major problem that arose in implementing Title II was the phrase, "to extend and to improve." Considerable pressure was brought on the Office of Education to give this an exceedingly broad interpretation which would allow the new funds to be used to replace trade and industrial funds made available under the Vocational Education Act of 1946, Title I, which had previously been used for practical nurse training. Since the act would not have been effective without this limitation, policies were developed by the Division of Vocational Education to define this phrase.

Apart from the value of encouraging extension and improvement, the language resulted in almost two distinct programs with consequent difficulties of reporting and fiscal accounting. In view of this, and in view of the belief that states would continue to promote the program without the restriction for extension and improvement, the act was later amended.

VOCATIONAL EDUCATION IN THE FISHING INDUSTRY[5]

The purpose of this act was to "promote the fishing industry in the United States and its Territories by providing for the training of needed personnel for such industries."

The act authorized the appropriation of $372,000 for vocational education in the fishery trades and industry and distributive occupations therein. An appropriation of $180,000 has been made each year. The act provided that the amounts appropriated were to be apportioned between states and territories on an equitable basis as determined by the U. S. Commissioner of Education after consultation with the Secretary of Interior, taking into account the extent of the fishing industry in each state and territory as compared with the total fishing industry in the United States. The program under this act has developed substantively in only a few of the coastal states.

TITLE III OF GEORGE-BARDEN ACT. AREA VOCATIONAL SCHOOLS, PROGRAMS FOR THE EDUCATION OF TECHNICIANS[6]

This act was titled "The National Defense Education Act of 1958." Title VIII of the act amended the Vocational Education

---

[5] Public Law 84–1027, 84th Congress, 2nd Session; S. 2379, approved August 8, 1956.

[6] Public Law 85–864, 85th Congress, 2nd Session; H.R. 13247, approved September 2, 1958.

Act of 1946 by adding to it a Title III, "Area Vocational Education Programs." This amendment provided for area vocational education programs to meet national defense needs for highly skilled technicians and authorized an appropriation of $15,000,000 annually until June 30, 1962.

The area concept in vocational education, that vocational schools should be established to serve more than one school district, had been evolving for a number of years. Unsuccessful efforts were made to include provision for such special schools in the Vocational Education Act of 1946. A bill (S. 4301) was introduced in the 84th Congress relative to the establishment of area vocational schools and programs and comparable separate legislation was introduced early in the 85th Congress. When the sponsors of the National Defense Education Act introduced their bills, the proposal concerning area vocational education was included.

This title was in and out of the bill during its consideration. The Governors' Committee on Federal-State Relations appointed in 1957, recommended that vocational education support from federal funds be limited to programs which were clearly identifiable as necessary for national defense. When the NDEA bill was being considered in the Senate it was amended to accomplish this by adding to Title VIII, Section 303:

(3) That funds appropriated under Section 301 of this title be used exclusively for the training of individuals designed to fit them for useful employment as highly skilled technicians in recognized occupations requiring scientific knowledge as determined by the State board for such State in fields necessary for the national defense.

After approval of the National Defense Education Act, the Division of Vocational Education, Office of Education, secured the services of several consultants who were authorities in the field of technical education and developed a draft of regulations. Representatives of many organizations considered as having an interest in this new type of program were invited to a meeting where the legislation was explained.

Some representatives of labor feared that the program was designed to train single skill workers such as had been trained during World War II, but who could not qualify as journeymen. Some groups in the educational field felt that this was a type of training which vocational education was not prepared or suitably equipped to provide, and that it might more appropriately be given by colleges. Objections to the program were also raised by representatives of a group of private technical institutes who feared that they could not meet the competition of a publicly supported program. The fears of all these groups were eventually allayed to the extent that they saw fit to cooperate in the program and on a number of occasions have served in advisory capacities. Regulations were clarified, a close working relationship established with industry, and effective programs were developed on both a preparatory and an extension basis.

VOCATIONAL EDUCATION ACTS APPLIED TO STATE OF ALASKA[7]

This act is cited as the "Alaska Omnibus Act." The legislation amended Section 4 of the Smith-Hughes Act of February 23, 1917, to increase from $90,000 to $98,500 the annual appropriation used to supplement the $1,000,000 basic annual appropriation for teacher training, thereby assuring the specified minimum allotment to each state. The requirement in the Smith-Hughes Act, that not more than 60 per cent nor less than 20 per cent of the money allotted to a state for teacher training should be used to train teachers in any one vocational field was made inapplicable to Alaska for a period of three years. P. L. 86-70 also amended the Vocational Education Act of 1946 and the National Defense Education Act of 1958 to refer to Alaska as a state rather than a territory.

VOCATIONAL EDUCATION ACTS APPLIED TO STATE OF HAWAII[8]

The act, known as the "Hawaii Omnibus Act," repealed Section 4 of the act of March 10, 1924, which extended benefits of the Smith-Hughes Act to Hawaii. It also amended Sections 2 and 4 of the Smith-Hughes Act to increase the appropriation for providing annual minimums to states for salaries of teachers of vocational

---

[7] Public Law 86–70, 86th Congress, 1st Session; H.R. 7120, approved June 25, 1959.

[8] Public Law 86–624, 86th Congress, 2nd Session; H.R. 11602, approved July 12, 1960.

agriculture from $27,000 to $28,000, and for teacher training from $98,500, provided for in the Public Law Amendment, to $105,200. The act also amended the Vocational Education Act of 1946 to refer to Hawaii as a state rather than as a territory.

EXTENSION OF GEORGE-BARDEN ACT, TITLE II. PRACTICAL NURSE TRAINING[9]

The Health Amendments Act of 1956 (P.L. 911, 84th Congress) added Title II to the Vocational Education Act of 1946, authorizing an appropriation not to exceed $5,000,000 for the fiscal year ending June 30, 1957, and for each of the next four fiscal years, for the purpose of extending and improving practical nurse training. P.L. 87-22 extended this appropriation authorization an additional four years, to June 30, 1965, and deleted the phrase requiring extension and improvement.

AREA REDEVELOPMENT ACT, VOCATIONAL EDUCATION PROVISION[10]

The purpose of the "Area Redevelopment Act" is to establish a four year program to alleviate conditions of substantial and persistent unemployment and underemployment in certain economically distressed areas. Section 16 of the act provides for vocational training and retraining of unemployed and underemployed persons in recognized redevelopment areas. The Secretary of Labor has responsibility under the act to determine the occupations for which training is to be given, to select the persons to be trained, and to place them when trained. The amount of $4,500,000 is authorized for appropriation annually to the Department of Labor. Amounts are transferred to the Department of Health, Education, and Welfare for costs of administering the training program and for payments to states for costs of conducting the training.

Section 16 also provides that the training is to be given by the appropriate state vocational educational agency, except that when such agency does not see fit to do so, the Secretary of Health, Education, and Welfare may contract with public or private educational institutions to give the training. All costs directly attributable to the training may be paid from federal funds.

---

[9] Public Law 87–22, 87th Congress, 1st Session; S. 278, approved April 24, 1961.

[10] Public Law 87–27, 87th Congress, 1st Session. S. 1; approved May 1, 1961.

Sections 16 and 17 of this law have been replaced by Public Law 89-15, Title II, Part C, Section 241. The same services continue to be provided but are now provided under this new law (approved April 26, 1965), which is an extension of the Manpower Development and Training Act of 1962.

EXTENSION OF GEORGE-BARDEN ACT, TITLE III.
AREA VOCATIONAL SCHOOLS, PROGRAMS FOR
THE EDUCATION OF TECHNICIANS[11]

Title II of this act amended Title VIII of the National Defense Education Act of 1958, and Title III of the Vocational Education Act of 1964, by extending the provisions for area vocational education programs for two years, from June 30, 1962, to June 30, 1964. Title VIII of the National Defense Education Act of 1958 had amended the Vocational Education Act of 1964 by adding to it a Title II, "Area Vocational Education Programs."

In the fifteen year period from 1947 to 1961, eleven federal laws were enacted relating to vocational education. Federal funds directed to states for vocational education increased from about 22 million dollars ($21,768,000—1946-'47) to about 50 million dollars ($49,842,000—1960-'61) during this period. This was a very significant increase in federal support of vocational education. But the enrollment in public high schools almost doubled during the same period and increasing costs reduced the purchasing power of the dollar appreciably during these years. The effective federal support of vocational education therefore did not increase. At the same time, however, the state and local funds for vocational education more than tripled (from 62 million dollars in 1946-'47 to 206 million dollars in 1960-'61), and this did not include the funds spent for buildings and equipment by state and local governments.

Of the eleven federal laws approved in these fifteen years, seven were amendments or extensions of existing laws. Four were new laws bringing about major changes in federal involvement in vocational education.

Three of the four new laws provided designated funds for new categories of vocational education (Practical Nurse Training,

---

[11] Public Law 87–344, 87th Congress, 1st Session. S. 2393, approved October 3, 1961.

Technician Training, and Training for the Fishing Industry). These new categories, added to the existing four categories (Agriculture, Trade and Industry, Home Economics, and Distribution), made seven categories for which specified amounts of federal funds were available. Educational programs for these new occupational categories had been in operation in many states for years under the general category of Trade and Industrial Education. It might be inferred from this legislation that Congress felt vocational education programs in these categories were not adequate.

The fourth major part of the new legislation for vocational education during this period was *Section 16* of the *Area Redevelopment Act*. This legislation set out to redevelop certain distressed or substandard urban areas and to alleviate conditions of substantial and persistent unemployment and underemployment. The funds to be used for training were allocated to the Department of Labor. This department determined the employment needs and the persons available and eligible for training. The administration and operation of the training programs were to be a responsibility of state vocational agencies. This division of responsibility and multi-agency involvement was a new feature of federal legislation for vocational education. Much of the federal legislation approved in later years followed this pattern of multi-agency responsibility.

During the decade 1950-1960, attempts were made to eliminate federal participation in vocational education programs. Legislation was introduced to gradually abolish the acts over a six-year period. Funds for distributive education were severely cut with the result that enrollment in distributive education courses dropped by more than 100,000 during a one-year period. Various commissions and committees recommended that the federal government completely withdraw financial support for vocational education. These recommendations were not intended primarily as a criticism of vocational education programs; rather they reflected a prevailing philosophy that the states and local communities should pay for vocational education programs, as well as for other activities to which the federal government was contributing through grants to the states.

It is highly significant that none of these recommendations resulted in any permanent decrease of federal support. Instead, Congress overwhelmingly supported increased appropriations for

vocational education. Even though funds for distributive education were cut, Congress refused to completely eliminate aid for this
program. In general, the debates in Congress indicate almost universal support for vocational education. No specific criticism was
made by any member of Congress as to the value of vocational
education; on the contrary, members of both the House and Senate
vigorously defended the programs. One representative said that
"the vocational education program, operated under state and local
supervision and control, has never been the subject of a breath of
scandal. The words graft, waste, and inefficiency have never attached themselves, even by innuendo, to its dedicated teaching and
administrative staffs." [12]

[12] *Congressional Record,* June 9, 1954, pg. 7950.

CHAPTER X

Federal Legislation for Vocational-Technical
Education Since 1961

The best evidence of congressional interest in vocational-technical education is the large number of acts which have been approved during the last four years. From 1900 through 1959, 60 years, seventeen federal acts were approved which remain in effect. In the past four years, twenty-five acts have been approved. These trends in federal vocational education legislation are illustrated in Table I. Much of the recent legislation is quite different from the legislation of the earlier years.

It was relatively easy to outline and categorize federal legislation for vocational education prior to 1960. With very few exceptions the legislation provided funds for the United States Office of Education to distribute to the various states to subsidize vocational education programs operated by local school districts. It allocated funds for specific occupational categories and provided definite limiting factors. The federal funds had to be matched by the state and local school districts.

Beginning in 1962 and extending through the more recent congressional sessions, the conditions have been quite different. Some of the newer provisions had antecedents in prior legislation but, in general, the following provisions became common features of federal laws related to manpower development only since 1961.

1. Occupational categories are not specified.

2. Severe detailed restrictive limitations have been eliminated.

3. A close relationship between labor market needs, course content, and numbers in training is required.

4. State and local matching funds are not always required.

5. Multi-agency responsibilities at the federal level are not uncommon.

6. Agencies other than state and local schools may be involved.

7. Provisions for research, experimentation, and pilot projects are permitted, encouraged, and often required.

8. Evaluation and detailed reporting are mandated.

9. Ancillary services and programs are permitted and often required.

10. Private schools have been opened for federally subsidized vocational training programs.

11. Basic education subjects (reading, writing and arithmetic) have been made a part of vocational education to persons where the lack of such skills severely handicaps employment.

12. Financial support to the trainee has been provided during the period of training.

13. Federal funds have been allocated for the purchase of supplies, equipment, and the construction or renovation of buildings.

14. A greater emphasis on vocational-technical education beyond the high school. Automation and mechanization within business, agriculture and industry are demanding skills and knowledge which require time and maturity beyond that of the high school student. Junior colleges, technical institutes and even some four-year colleges are providing such educational programs.

The following tabulations are presented in order to illustrate the great diversity of activities which are now supported by federal legislation and related to manpower development. The programs are so diversified and interrelated that it is impossible to outline clearly and simply the present situation. It is believed, however, that this inventory of federal legislation which is now in effect is an accurate statement even though it is not complete and is not always consistent with other tabulations.

A number of federal laws have been temporary—such as the legislation providing for vocational education for national defense during World War II. Other federal legislation has been superseded by later legislation—George-Reed Act of 1929, superseded by the George-Ellzey Act of 1934, superseded by the George-Dean Act of 1936, superseded by the George-Barden Act of 1946.

Legislation which is not now in effect is not listed in these tabulations.[1]

As one examines these data it becomes apparent that the recent legislation exhibits a diversity which is quite different from

---

[1] Much of the material in these tabulations was taken from a *Staff Paper* of the U.S. Department of Labor, "Inventory of Federally-Assisted Manpower Development Programs." Office of Manpower, Automation and Training, Division of Manpower Program Planning, August 24, 1965. 25 pages, mimeographed.

TABLE I. FEDERAL LEGISLATION APPROVED SINCE 1900 WHICH ASSISTS MANPOWER DEVELOPMENT

DECADE	NUMBER OF LEGISLATIVE ACTS	PUBLIC LAW DESIGNATION		
1900–1909	0	0		
1910–1919	1	64–347		
1920–1929	2	67–85,	66–236	
1930–1939	3	(73–245)*,	(74–672)*,	75–308
1940–1949	3	78–16,	78–410,	79–586
1950–1959	11	81–507 82–550 83–565	83–703 84–634 84–959	85–568 85–864 85–926
1960–1965	30	87–256 87–276 87–344 87–415 87–510 87–543 87–729 87–794 87–838 88–129	88–164 88–204 88–206 88–210 88–214 88–352 88–452 88–497 88–581 88–605	88–654 88–660 88–665 89–4 89–10 89–15 89–36 89–105 89–287 89–290

*THESE ACTS HAVE BEEN REPLACED BY THE GEORGE–BARDEN ACT OF 1946, P. L. 79–586.

the legislation of the first half of this century. As one studies this legislation the trends mentioned earlier are readily detected.

THE PANEL OF CONSULTANTS ON VOCATIONAL EDUCATION

President Kennedy in his message to Congress on February 20, 1961, said:

The National Vocational Education Acts, first enacted by the Congress in 1917 and subsequently amended, have provided a program of training for industry, agriculture, and other occupational areas. The basic purpose of our vocational effort is sound and sufficiently broad to provide a basis for meeting future needs. However, the technological changes which have occurred in all occupations call for a review and re-evaluation of these Acts, with a view toward their modernization.

To that end, I am requesting the Secretary of Health, Education, and Welfare to convene an advisory body drawn from the educational profession, labor-industry, and agriculture, as well as the lay public, together with representation from the Departments of Agriculture and Labor, to be charged with the responsibility of reviewing and evaluating the current National Vocational Education Acts, and making recommendations for improving and redirecting the program.

The advisory committee was appointed by the Secretary of Health, Education and Welfare and announced by the White

House on October 5, 1961. This action emulated that of the Congress and the President in appointing the Commission on National Aid to Vocational Education in 1914.[2]

This committee was called *The Panel of Consultants on Vocational Education*. The panel was chosen to be representative of many facets of education, business, and labor, from many sections of the country.

The members of the committee met eight times from November, 1961 to November, 1962. They had a full-time staff of six persons directed by J. Chester Swanson, Professor of Educational Administration, University of California, Berkeley. In November, 1962 they were received by President Kennedy and presented to him a report recommending major changes in federal legislation for vocational-technical education.[3] Their recommendations were largely incorporated into a proposed bill which became the Vocational Education Act of 1963.

PANEL MEMBERS

Mrs. Mary Caperton Bingham
Louisville Courier-Journal
Louisville, Kentucky

Dr. Hyman Bookbinder
Special Assistant to the Secretary
U.S. Department of Commerce
Washington, D.C.

Hon. Charles F. Carroll
Superintendent of Public Instruction
North Carolina, and
President, Council of Chief School
Officers
Raleigh, North Carolina

Mr. Frederick T. Corleto
Corleto Buick Agency
South Philadelphia, Pennsylvania

Mr. Henry A. Gonzales
State Supervisor of Trade and
Industrial Education
State Department of Education
Santa Fe, New Mexico

Dr. Francis A. Gregory
Assistant Superintendent and
Director of Vocational Education
District of Columbia Public Schools
Washington, D.C.

Mr. Floyd D. Johnson
Teacher of Vocational Agriculture
York Public Schools
York, South Carolina

Dr. Helen R. LeBaron
Dean, College of Home Economics
Iowa State University
Ames, Iowa

---

[2] See: Chapter V.

[3] *Education for a Changing World of Work*, Report of the Panel of Consultants on Vocational Education. Department of Health, Education, and Welfare.
    Full report—*Publication OE-80021*, 296 pp., 1963
    Summary report—*Publication OE-80020*, 24 pp., 1962
    U.S. Government Printing Office, Washington, D.C.

Mr. Ernest H. Dean
Industrial Coordinator
 Central Utah Vocational School,
and Speaker,
House of Representatives, Utah

Dr. Mark Ellingson
President
Rochester Institute of Technology
Rochester, New York

Mrs. Margaret C. Ells
Scholarship Counselor
American International College
Springfield, Massachusetts

Mr. Charles W. Engelhard, Jr.
Chairman of the Board
Engelhard Industries
Newark, New Jersey

Dr. Edward B. Evans
President
Prairie View Agricultural and
 Mechanical College
Prairie View, Texas

Mr. Thomas H. Quigley
Professor, and Head,
 Industrial Education Department
Georgia Institute of Technology
Atlanta, Georgia

Mrs. Helen Radke
President
National School Boards Association
Port Angeles, Washington

Mr. Peter T. Schoemann
President
United Association of Journeymen and
Apprentices of the Plumbing and
Pipefitting Industry
Washington, D.C.

Dr. Paul H. Sheats
Dean, University Extension
University of California
Los Angeles, California

Dr. William B. Logan
Professor of Education
Ohio State University,
and President,
American Vocational Association
Columbus, Ohio

Mr. Charles Odell
Director of Retired and Older
 Workers Department,
International Union of the United Auto
 Workers
Detroit, Michigan

Mr. James Patton
President
National Farmers Union
Denver, Colorado

Mr. J. B. Perky
Director of Vocational Education
State Department of Education
Stillwater, Oklahoma

Dr. Benjamin C. Willis
Superintendent of Schools
Board of Education
City of Chicago
Chicago, Illinois

Dr. Seymour L. Wolfbein
Deputy Assistant
Secretary of Labor,
U.S. Department of Labor
Washington, D.C.

Dr. Dael Wolfle
Executive Officer
American Association for the
 Advancement of Science
Washington, D.C.

Dr. E. T. York
Director
Federal Extension Service
U.S. Department of Agriculture
Washington, D.C.

FEDERAL LEGISLATION PROVIDING FUNDS TO STATE AGENCIES TO SUBSIDIZE VOCATIONAL-TECHNICAL EDUCATION PROGRAMS OPERATED BY STATE AND LOCAL SCHOOL DISTRICTS. 1962 to 1965.

The Vocational Education Act of 1963. Essentially, the Vocational Education Act of 1963[4] is the same type of legislation as the Smith-Hughes Act of 1917 and the George-Barden Act of 1946. It may be considered an extension of these acts. It does not replace earlier legislation although it does modify the two earlier acts in several ways.

The act authorizes a new permanent program with considerable increase of authorized appropriations. The funds appropriated for fiscal year 1965 were as follows:

Smith-Hughes Act of 1917	**$ 7,161,455**
George-Barden Act of 1946	**49,990,823**
Vocational Education Act of 1963	**118,500,000**
TOTAL	**$175,652,278**

With the present authorizations in effect these appropriations could be as follows for fiscal year 1967 and thereafter:

Smith-Hughes Act of 1917	**$ 7,161,455**
George-Barden Act of 1946	**49,990,823**
Vocational Education Act of 1963	**225,000,000**
TOTAL	**$282,152,278**

The major provisions of the Vocational Education Act of 1963 might be outlined as follows:

1. Specifies no occupational categories, but designates that business and office occupations be included.
2. Broadens definition of vocational and technical education.
3. Permits the use of federal funds to support the purchase of equipment and the construction of buildings.
4. Makes Title II (Practical Nurse Training) and Title III (Area Technical Training School Programs) of George-

---

[4] Public Law 88–210, 88th Congress, 1st Session; approved December 18, 1963.

Barden Act of 1946 permanent with continuing authorizations of $5,000,000 and $15,000,000 per year, respectively.

5. Requires a cooperation between state vocational agencies and state employment services.
6. Requires periodic review of administration and programs at the state and federal levels.
7. Makes changes in the Smith-Hughes Act of 1917 and the George-Barden Act of 1946.
   a. Allows transfer of funds from one occupational category to another.
   b. Broadens definition of vocational agriculture programs.
   c. Permits pre-employment training in distributive education.
   d. Removes requirement for nine-months minimum programs and fifty percent of school time in vocational programs.
   e. States that vocational home economics students may train for gainful employment in occupations involving knowledge and skills in home economics subjects, and requires that at least 10 percent of such funds provided in earlier acts be used for such purposes.
8. Authorization is given for the appropriation of funds for work-study programs and residential vocational education schools ($50,000,000 in fiscal year 1966).
9. Ten percent of the funds appropriated under the Vocational Education Act of 1963 are reserved for grants to be used for research, experimental, and developmental programs.

This legislation will have a major impact on vocational-technical education in high schools, vocational schools, technical institutes, and community colleges. The increased funds will produce more programs; the broadened definition and lowered restrictions will promote innovations in curriculums; and the research activities and periodic review will focus attention on quality factors.

TABLE II. FEDERAL LEGISLATION ASSISTING VOCATIONAL–TECHNICAL EDUCATION
PROGRAMS OPERATED BY STATE AND LOCAL SCHOOLS
FOR FISCAL YEAR 1965

FEDERAL LEGISLATION	NO. OF PERSONS	EXPENDITURES*
SMITH–HUGHES ACT OF 1917, P. L. 64-347, AS AMENDED		$ 7,161,455
GEORGE–BARDEN ACT OF 1946, P. L. 79-586, AS AMENDED	5,300,000	49,990,823
VOCATIONAL EDUCATION ACT OF 1963, P. L. 88-210		118,500,000
NATIONAL APPRENTICESHIP LAW OF 1937, P. L. 75-308	170,500	NO FUNDS TO THE LOCAL SCHOOL DISTRICTS
AREA REDEVELOPMENT ACT OF 1961, P. L. 87-27	11,078	6,700,000**
MANPOWER DEVELOPMENT AND TRAINING ACT OF 1962, P. L. 87-415 AND 87-729 AS AMENDED	214,089	280,300,000***
TRADE EXPANSION ACT OF 1962 P. L. 87-794		NO APPROPRIATIONS
TOTAL	5,695,667	$462,652,278

*THE EXPENDITURE FIGURES ARE EITHER ACTUAL EXPENDITURES OR ESTIMATES BASED ON EXPENDITURES FOR A MAJOR PART OF THE YEAR.

**THE ADMINISTRATION OF THESE FUNDS WAS A JOINT RESPONSIBILITY OF THE U.S. DEPARTMENT OF COMMERCE, THE U.S. DEPARTMENT OF LABOR, AND THE OFFICE OF EDUCATION OF THE U.S. DEPARTMENT OF HEALTH, EDUCATION, AND WELFARE. ONLY A SMALL PERCENTAGE OF THIS AMOUNT WENT TO LOCAL SCHOOL DISTRICTS TO COVER THE VOCATIONAL EDUCATION PERFORMED UNDER THIS ACT.

***THE ADMINISTRATION OF THESE FUNDS WAS A JOINT RESPONSIBILITY OF THE U.S. DEPARTMENT OF LABOR AND THE OFFICE OF EDUCATION OF THE U.S. DEPARTMENT OF HEALTH, EDUCATION, AND WELFARE. ONLY A SMALL PERCENTAGE OF THIS AMOUNT WENT TO LOCAL SCHOOL DISTRICTS TO COVER THE VOCATIONAL EDUCATION PERFORMED UNDER THIS ACT.

FEDERAL LEGISLATION PROVIDING FUNDS FOR MANPOWER DEVELOPMENT AND TRAINING PROGRAMS INVOLVING OTHER FEDERAL OR STATE AGENCIES IN ADDITION TO VOCATIONAL EDUCATION DIVISIONS OF STATE GOVERNMENT. 1962-1965.

In 1937 Congress approved The National Apprenticeship Law (the Fitzgerald Act[5]) which gave rise to the Bureau of Apprenticeship and Training in the Department of Labor. The department received the appropriations and provided assistance throughout

---

[5] Public Law 75–308, 75th Congress, 1st Session; approved August 16, 1937.

the nation in promoting apprenticeship programs and maintaining quality standards. Related training is required of all apprentices and this related training is usually provided by local school districts, using local, state, and federal vocational education funds.

TABLE III. FEDERAL LEGISLATION ASSISTING MANPOWER DEVELOPMENT PROGRAMS
FOR GROUPS WITH SPECIAL NEEDS

FOR FISCAL YEAR 1965

FEDERAL LEGISLATION	NO. OF PERSONS	EXPENDITURES
VETERANS VOCATIONAL REHABILITATION ACT OF 1943, P. L. 78-16	7,639	$ 14,500,000
VETERANS READJUSTMENT ASSISTANCE ACT OF 1952, P. L. 82-550	18,253	11,800,000 (11 MOS.)
VOCATIONAL REHABILITATION AMENDMENTS OF 1954, P. L. 83-565	88,301	24,300,000 (EST.)
WAR ORPHANS EDUCATIONAL ASSISTANCE ACT OF 1956, P. L. 84-634	23,257	25,600,000
ADULT INDIAN VOCATIONAL TRAINING ACT OF 1956, P. L. 84-959	4,961	9,300,000 (11 MOS.)
MIGRATION AND REFUGEE ASSISTANCE ACT OF 1962, P. L. 87-510 (A) ADULT VOCATIONAL EDUCATION AND ENGLISH	10,000	1,300,000
CIVIL RIGHTS ACT OF 1964 TITLES IV AND VI, P. L. 88-352	NOT KNOWN	8,000,000
ECONOMIC OPPORTUNITY ACT OF 1964 P. L. 88-452		
(A) TITLE 1-A, JOB CORPS	31,000	183,000,000
(B) TITLE 1-B, WORK TRAINING PROGRAM	278,000	132,500,000
(C) TITLE 1-C, WORK STUDY PROGRAMS	83,000	56,000,000
(D) TITLE II-B, ADULT BASIC EDUCATION PROGRAMS	35,000	19,000,000
(E) TITLE III-B, ASSISTANCE FOR MIGRANTS	10,000	2,000,000
(F) TITLE V, WORK EXPERIENCE PROGRAMS	88,700	112,000,000
SUBTOTAL	525,700	$504,500,000
APPALACHIAN REGIONAL DEVELOPMENT ACT OF 1965, P. L. 89-4	NOT EFFECTIVE IN F. Y. 1965	
NATIONAL TECHNICAL INSTITUTES FOR THE DEAF ACT OF 1965, P.L. 89-36	NOT EFFECTIVE IN F. Y. 1965	
TOTAL	658,111	$599,300,000

NOTE. THIS TABLE DOES NOT INCLUDE VOCATIONAL TRAINING IN CORRECTIONAL INSTITUTIONS OR THE PROGRAMS UNDER THE MANPOWER, TRAINING AND DEVELOPMENT ACT WHICH SERVE GROUPS WITH SPECIAL NEEDS.

Immediately prior to and during World War II, extensive vocational training was performed in which the federal government paid the total costs. The training programs were operated by the local schools in close cooperation with the Department of Labor.

The Area Redevelopment Act of 1961.[6] This act established a program to alleviate conditions of substantial and persistent unemployment and underemployment in certain economically distressed areas. It required that the U. S. Department of Commerce determine the degree of distress and the U. S. Department of Labor certify to the need for training. It also required that the state employment services determine who might benefit from training and what job opportunities existed. The training program and the trainee were then referred to a local school district to establish and operate the training program. The federal government paid all the costs.

This trend toward joint responsibility for manpower development programs and the payment of the total cost by the federal government were salient features of an act known as MDTA.

The Manpower Development and Training Act of 1962 (MDTA).[7] This legislation authorizes the Secretary of Labor to appraise the manpower requirements and resources of the nation and, working with the Secretary of Health, Education, and Welfare and with state agencies, to provide training programs for the unemployed and underemployed. The Department of Labor with the state employment services determines the employment needs and the potential trainees. These programs have been funded 100 percent by the federal government. After June 30, 1966 the federal funds may not be more than 90 per cent of the costs. The non-federal contributions may be in cash or kind.

The Department of Health, Education, and Welfare, through the U. S. Office of Education, Bureau of Adult and Vocational Education, Division of Vocational and Technical Education, provided for the training programs through the state vocational agencies.

---

[6] Public Law 87–27, 87th Congress, 1st Session; approved May 1, 1961. Amended by Public Law 89–15, 89th Congress, 1st Session; approved April 26, 1965.

[7] Public Law 87–415, 87th Congress, 2nd Session; approved March 15, 1962.

The vocational-technical training utilizes the same administrative channels as established by the Smith-Hughes and George-Barden Acts. However, training is provided by a project method requiring federal approval for each project. It is administratively and financially efficient in that it generally uses existing management, facilities, and equipment.

This act provides for more than the previous vocational education acts in that it grants training allowances to certain eligible trainees and is related to national economic needs. The act has been expanded and extended by each legislative session, since the original approval. One of these amendments makes the training provisions of the Area Redevelopment Act a part of the Manpower Development and Training Act.[8]

The Economic Opportunity Act of 1964.[9] The objective of this legislation is to mobilize the human and financial resources of the nation to combat poverty in the United States. It attempts to achieve this objective by developing employable skills, and providing experiences and conditions to motivate those less fortunate persons in our society.

Very little of the training for persons receiving assistance from this act is performed by the local school districts, or administered by the state vocational agency, or the U. S. Department of Labor or the U. S. Department of Health, Education and Welfare.

The vocational training activities of this act are summarized as follows:

1. *The Job Corps*[10] provides for the establishment of rural or urban residential vocational schools whose objective is to prepare youths (age 16 through 21) for the responsibility of citizenship and to increase their employability. General education vocational training, work experience, and counseling are provided in each Corps location.

A Corps center is often under the direction of an industrial

---

[8] Public Law 89–15, 89th Congress, 1st Session, approved April 26 ,1965.

[9] Public Law 88–452, 88th Congress, 2nd Session, approved August 20th, 1964 and amended by Public Law 89–253, 89th Congress, 1st Session.

[10] P. L. 88–452, Title I-A

organization. As soon as a corpsman has achieved employable skills he is placed in a job by the state employment service.[11]

2. *Work-Training Programs* provide useful work experience opportunities for youth through participation in state and community work. Public or private non-profit agencies provide the work experience opportunities. Such work programs are geared to the public interest, often related to conservation, development of natural resources, or recreational areas.

3. *Work-Study Programs*[12] are organized for students in institutions of higher education who are from homes of low income families and are in need of the earnings from such employment to pursue courses of study at such institutions.

4. *The Adult Basic Education Program*[13] provides instruction for individuals who have attained an age of 18 or over, and whose inability to read and write the English language constitutes a substantial impairment of their ability to get or retain employment commensurate with their real ability.

5. *A Program to Assist Migrant and Seasonally Employed Agricultural Employees*[14] is provided by assisting states, political subdivisions of states, or public and non-profit agencies in establishing such programs.

6. *Work-Experience Programs*[15] are developed to expand the opportunities for constructive work experience and other needed training available to persons who are unable to support or care for themselves or their families. These programs must make maximum use of the activities under the Manpower Development and Training Act and the Vocational Educational Acts.

These programs are expected to provide assistance to more than 500,000 persons in 1966 and may have an appropriation of more than one billion dollars.

Trade Expansion Act of 1962.[16] The Trade Expansion Act of 1962 is very similar to the Area Redevelopment Act of 1961 in that it recognizes that certain changes may result from the

---

[11] P. L. 88–452, Title I-B

[12] P. L. 88–452, Title I-C

[13] P. L. 88–452, Title II-B

[14] P. L. 88–452, Title III-B

[15] P. L. 88–452, Title V

[16] Public Law 87–794, 87th Congress, 2nd Session; approved October 11, 1962.

economic dislocations from trade expansion, and that the persons who may be affected could be helped by vocational education. Sub-chapter B, Section 126, provides that testing, counseling, training, and placement services may be provided. It permits supplemental assistance such as transportation to the location of the training and subsistence during the period of training.

This act has not been implemented in many respects at this date, and thus no vocational training has been given under its provisions.

National Technical Institute for the Deaf Legislation.[17] Congress passed legislation in 1965 to provide for the establishment and operation of a residential facility for post-secondary technical training and education to prepare the deaf for successful employment. This school has not been constructed as of this date and is not yet in operation.

FEDERAL LEGISLATION PROVIDING FUNDS FOR THE CONSTRUCTION OF BUILDINGS FOR VOCATIONAL-TECHNICAL INSTRUCTION. 1962-65

A number of recent federal acts provide funds which may be used for the construction of facilities for vocational-technical instruction.

The Vocational Education Act of 1963[18] provides (in Section 4 (a) (5)) funds to be used for "the construction of area vocational education school facilities." The same funds can be used for program operation, and in practice these funds are much more likely to be used for operation than for construction. However, forty percent of the funds available in fiscal year 1966 are going for construction.

The Appalachian Regional Act of 1965[19] provides in Section 211 that vocational education facilities may be constructed from funds approved for this section—$16,000,000 may be available in 1966. This is a recent act and has not been fully implemented. However, one school has been approved for Georgia and sixteen have been approved for Kentucky.

---

[17] Public Law 89–36, 89th Congress, 1st Session; approved June 8, 1965.

[18] Public Law 88–210.

[19] Public Law 89–4, 89th Congress, 1st Session; approved March 9, 1965.

TABLE IV. FEDERAL LEGISLATION ASSISTING MANPOWER DEVELOPMENT PROGRAMS—
HIGHER EDUCATION AND PROFESSIONAL TRAINING

FOR FISCAL YEAR 1965

FEDERAL LEGISLATION	NO. OF PERSONS	EXPENDITURES
A. TEACHER TRAINING		
NATIONAL SCIENCE FOUNDATION ACT OF 1950, P. L. 81-507 AS AMENDED	46,262	$ 48,700,000
EDUCATIONAL AND CULTURAL EXCHANGE ACT OF 1961, P.L. 87-256, SEC. 102 (B) (6)	305	1,500,000
NATIONAL DEFENSE EDUCATION ACT OF 1958, (TITLES IV, V, VI-A, AND XI) P. L. 85-864 AS AMENDED	29,958	75,300,000
TRAINING TEACHERS FOR THE DEAF 1961, P.L. 87-276	432	1,000,000
TRAINING TEACHERS FOR THE HANDI-CAPPED 1965, P.L. 89-105	NOT EFFECTIVE IN F. Y. 1965	
SUBTOTAL	76,955	$126,500,000
B. HEALTH SERVICE OCCUPATIONS		
PUBLIC HEALTH SERVICE ACT OF 1944 P.L. 78-410, AS AMENDED, P.L. 84-911, PRACTICAL NURSE TRAINING, INCLUDED UNDER TITLE II OF P.L. 79-586 P. L. 87-838, 88-497		
FELLOWSHIPS	4,930	$ 46,808,000
TRAINEESHIPS	29,510	197,700,000
CLEAN AIR ACT OF 1963, P.L. 88-206		
FELLOWSHIPS	38	200,000
TRAINEESHIPS	67	1,000,000
HEALTH PROFESSIONS EDUCATION ASSISTANCE ACT OF 1963, P. L. 88-129, 88-654, 89-290		
STUDENT LOANS	18,210	10,200,000
WATER POLLUTION CONTROL ACT OF 1964, P.L. 88-660		
FELLOWSHIPS	101	600,000
TRAINEESHIPS	246	2,000,000
NURSE TRAINING ACT OF 1964 P.L. 88-581		
STUDENT LOANS	10,100	3,100,000
TRAINEESHIPS	6,600	8,000,000

(Continued on following page)

TABLE IV. (Continued)

FEDERAL LEGISLATION	NO. OF PERSON	EXPENDITURES
DEPARTMENT OF LABOR AND DE-PARTMENT OF HEALTH, EDUCA-TION AND WELFARE APPROPRIA-TION ACT OF 1965, P.L. 88-605 TRAINEESHIPS AND TRAINEES	1,117	1,300,000
MENTAL RETARDATION FACILITIES AND COMMUNITY MENTAL HEALTH CENTERS CONSTRUCTION ACT OF 1963, TITLE III, P.L. 88-164 (AMENDS P.L. 85-926) TRAIN-ING IN THE EDUCATION OF MENTALLY RETARDED CHILDREN	3,000	3,000,000
SUBTOTAL	73,919	$273,808,000
C. TRAINING IN SPECIAL SKILLS SOCIAL SECURITY ACT OF 1935 P.L. 74-271, TITLE V, SEC. 409 AND SEC. 1115, AS AMENDED, 87-543 TRAINING SUBSISTENCE	22,100	32,800,000
NATIONAL SCIENCE FOUNDATION ACT OF 1950, P.L. 81-507	13,629	34,600,000
ATOMIC ENERGY ACT OF 1954, SEC. 31a. P.L. 83-703 FELLOWSHIPS AND TRAINEESHIPS INSTITUTES	469 1,070	2,700,000 1,100,000
NATIONAL AERONAUTIC AND SPACE ADMINISTRATION ACT OF 1958, P.L. 85-568 TRAINEESHIPS	3,132	20,000,000
VOCATIONAL REHABILITATION AMENDMENTS OF 1954, SEC. 4 (A) (C), P.L. 83-565 TRAINEESHIPS	3,750	9,400,000
SUBTOTAL	44,150	$100,600,000
D. STUDENT LOANS AND MISCELLAN-EOUS EDUCATIONAL PROGRAMS FOR INDIANS ACT OF 1921, P.L. 67-85	1,700	$1,200,000
NATIONAL DEFENSE EDUCATION ACT OF 1958 TITLE II, P.L. 85-864 AS AMENDED, 87-344, 88-210, 88-665 STUDENT LOANS	317,000	176,000,000

(Continued on following page)

TABLE IV. (Continued)

FEDERAL LEGISLATION	NO. OF PERSONS	EXPENDITURES
EDUCATIONAL AND CULTURAL EXCHANGE ACT OF 1961, P.L. 87-256 SCHOLARSHIPS	1, 182	3, 000, 000
MIGRATION AND REFUGEE ASSIST-ANCE ACT OF 1962, P.L. 87-510 STUDENT LOANS REFRESHER TRAINING	8, 000 649	2, 500, 000 400, 000
NATIONAL VOCATIONAL STUDENT LOAN INSURANCE ACT OF 1965, P.L. 89-287	NOT IN EFFECT, F. Y. 1965	
HIGHER EDUCATION FACILITIES ACT OF 1963, P.L. 88-204	COMPARABLE STATISTICS NOT AVAILABLE	
HIGHER EDUCATION ACT OF 1965, P.L. 89-329 SCHOLARSHIPS NATIONAL TEACHERS CORPS	NOT IN EFFECT, F.Y. 1965	
ELEMENTARY AND SECONDARY EDUCATION ACT OF 1965, P.L. 89-10 RESEARCH TRAINING OF RESEARCHERS LIBRARY RESOURCES STRENGTHENING LEADERSHIP RESOURCES OF STATE EDUCA-TIONAL AGENCIES	NOT IN EFFECT, F.Y. 1965	
SUBTOTAL	328, 531	$183, 100, 000
HIGHER EDUCATION TOTAL	523, 555	$684, 008, 000

The Higher Education Facilities Act of 1963[20] provides under Title I *"Grants for Construction of Undergraduate Academic Facilities."* This title not only permits the use of these funds for "junior colleges and technical institutes" but requires that "at least 22 percent of the funds allotted to a state be made available only to" such institutions. Title III of the act also provides for loans for the construction of buildings.

The Higher Education Act of 1965[21] amended the act of 1963 by extending the act and increasing available funds.

---

[20] Public Law 88–204, 88th Congress, 1st Session; approved December 16, 1963.

[21] Public Law 89–329, 89th Congress, 1st Session; approved November 8, 1965.

TABLE V. SUMMARY, FEDERAL LEGISLATION ASSISTING MANPOWER DEVELOPMENT PROGRAMS

FOR FISCAL YEAR 1965

CATEGORIES OF PROGRAMS	NO. OF PERSONS	EXPENDITURES
VOCATIONAL-TECHNICAL EDUCATION OPERATED BY STATE AND LOCAL SCHOOL DISTRICTS	5, 695, 667	$ 462, 652, 278
MANPOWER PROGRAMS FOR GROUPS WITH SPECIAL NEEDS	658, 111	599, 300, 000
HIGHER EDUCATION AND PROFESSIONAL TRAINING	523, 555	684, 008, 000
TEACHER TRAINING	76, 955	126, 500, 000
HEALTH SERVICE OCCUPATIONS	73, 919	273, 808, 000
TRAINING IN SPECIAL SKILLS	44, 150	100, 600, 000
STUDENT LOANS AND MISCELLANEOUS	328, 531	183, 100, 000
TOTAL	6, 877, 333	$1, 745, 960, 278

NOTE: THIS SUMMARY AND TOTALS MAY BE VERY MISLEADING BECAUSE MANY OF THE STATISTICAL REPORTS FROM WHICH THE INFORMATION WAS TAKEN CONTAIN DATA WHICH ARE NOT CONSISTENT.

FEDERAL LEGISLATION PROVIDING FUNDS FOR TEACHER TRAINING, FELLOWSHIPS, SCHOLAR-SHIPS, TRAINEESHIPS, OR STUDENT LOANS. 1962-1965.

Many federal acts include provisions for manpower development. These provisions are intended to enable the necessary number of persons to develop their skills and knowledge and to achieve the objective of the legislation. The acts include provisions for Fellowships, Scholarships, Traineeships or Loans to students. In most acts these provisions are created by a special title or section. Legislation with these provisions is outlined in Table VI. This legislation is often related to higher education institutions which provide the teacher training or other opportunities for skill development. Vocational-technical education teachers and technicians benefit from these training provisions.

Twenty-eight different federal legislative acts have been listed in this chapter as approved by Congress in the four-year period, 1962 to 1965. This is approximately the same number of legislative acts relating to vocational-technical education as approved in the previous sixty-year period. The federal government's increasing interest in vocational-technical education is most significant.

TABLE VI.   FEDERAL LEGISLATION PROVIDING FUNDS FOR TEACHER TRAINING, FELLOWSHIPS, SCHOLARSHIPS, TRAINEESHIPS OR LOANS TO STUDENTS—1962-1965

FEDERAL LEGISLATION TITLE	PUBLIC LAW NUMBER	SECTION OR SUBTITLE	ACTIVITY PROVIDED
VOC. ED. ACT, 1963	P.L. 88-210-A	SEC. 4 (A) (6)	TEACHER TRAINING
N.D.E.A. AMENDMENT	P.L. 88-665	TITLE V	COUNSELING AND GUIDANCE TRAINING
N.D.E.A. AMENDMENT	P.L. 88-665	TITLE II	LOANS TO STUDENTS
VOC. STUDENT LOAN INSURANCE ACT	P.L. 89-287		STUDENT LOAN INSURANCE
COMMUNITY MENTAL HEALTH CENTERS	P.L. 88-164	TITLE III	TEACHER TRAINING FELLOWSHIPS
HEALTH AMENDMENTS	P.L. 89-105		SCHOLARSHIPS TRAINEESHIPS
CIVIL RIGHTS ACT	P.L. 88-352	TITLE IV, SEC. 404	TEACHER TRAINING
CLEAN AIR ACT	P.L. 88-206		FELLOWSHIPS TRAINEESHIPS
NURSE TRAINING ACT	P.L. 88-581		TRAINEESHIPS STUDENT LOANS
SOCIAL SECURITY ACT AMENDMENT	P.L. 87-543	TITLE V	FELLOWSHIPS TRAINEESHIPS
PUBLIC HEALTH SERVICE ACT AMENDMENT	P.L. 87-838	SEC. 301	FELLOWSHIPS TRAINEESHIPS
HOUSING ACT OF 1964	P.L. 88-560	TITLE VIII	TRAINING FELLOWSHIPS

The federal government is no longer providing "seed money" to initiate vocational education programs. It is accepting a responsibility, jointly with state and local governments, to support vocational-technical education. Congress believes that the productive capacity of our nation and the welfare of our citizens can be appreciably improved by education and training related to labor market needs.

If the state and local educational leadership can use the funds now available and produce more effective manpower, and give more citizens economic security, then the future will see a general acceptance of manpower development through vocational education as a necessary and productive investment of government.